UnStuck

I've Found The Recipe For Being

Happy

JENNIFER RASH

Unstuck—I've Found The Recipe For Being Happy

Print book: 978-1-945464-81-2
eBook: 978-1-945464-82-9

Published by:
Jennifer Rash

Editor – Nikki Starnes

Cover design – Christine Dupre

Interior design – Lisa Thomson

DEDICATION

At the time I was writing this devotional book and study, one of my siblings was fighting for his life due to cancer. Maybe you've been there, too, wrestling physically, mentally, and emotionally, trying to find your feet again. To my brother Tom, all my siblings, and all of you—may you truly know and experience inner peace, true satisfaction, and contentment under all circumstances. May you find the true source of happiness. May you break free from every area of your life where you have felt stuck. And may you move forward with great purpose. Now is the time to live, really live!

CONTENTS

Chapter

INTRODUCTION

I've Found the Recipe for Being Happy

Is there a recipe for happiness regardless of what someone may have experienced in their past? Is there a recipe for happiness regardless of whether one's personal circumstances are favorable or unfavorable? The Apostle Paul seemed to think so. In fact, he not only believed it, but he also lived a life of continuous inner contentment and happiness. He was happy in spite of the conditions of his life. (And that is saying a lot considering who he was and what he endured!)

Paul was a true apostle in every sense. The man had a clear conscience and was blameless before the Lord. This faithful servant of God was willing to suffer for the sake of the Gospel, and suffer he did! The Apostle Paul had hard times, tough times, and bad times. The Bible tells us that he experienced hardships of every kind and was surrounded by troubles on every side. Many times, Paul labored and toiled to the point of exhaustion. And if that wasn't enough, he was frequently in circumstances that deprived him of his very basic needs: food, drink, and proper clothing. He knew what it was like to be hungry, thirsty, cold, and shivering. On many occasions, the Apostle Paul endured sleepless nights and was weary. His journeys brought difficulties too many to count. He faced constant dangers in his travels: dangers from rivers and robbers, dangers in cities and in deserts, dangers in the wilderness and on the seas. Once, Paul was bitten by a viper. At least three times he was shipwrecked. Paul spent an entire night and day adrift at sea. And like many of us, Paul knew what it was like to suffer from a physical condition. Scripture refers to his condition as the thorn in his side. It's described as an infirmity or a handicap, one which he prayed and prayed for God to take away from him. Having lost Barnabas, his close friend and ministry companion, Paul was also acquainted with sorrow and grief.

Even more painful than these hardships and "bad breaks" was the persecution he faced as he faithfully preached the gospel. He lived at constant risk for Jesus's sake. Paul was persecuted, flogged, whipped, and beaten within an inch of his life. Numerous times, he was arrested and thrown into prison. Often, he was confronted with situations that could have resulted in death. Once, he was stoned and left for dead. Paul was harassed, mistreated, mocked, and insulted. He found himself surrounded by angry mobs. This man was discredited, dishonored, blamed, and slandered. Evil reports were spoken against him. He was a faithful laborer for the cause of Christ, and yet he suffered and was treated like a nobody. Paul was driven out of cities he ministered in. He was plotted against by foes. He faced great opposition, struggling with not only his enemies but also his friends. Paul was betrayed even by those who would identify as believers and refer to themselves as his brothers. His own people, the Jews, stirred up trouble against him. There were times when Paul was simply perplexed and unsure of finding a way out.

The Apostle Paul was surrounded and battered by troubles, and on top of it all, he carried a heavy burden of responsibility for all the churches. There wasn't a day that went by that he didn't have a deep concern for the people. Yet, Paul described this heaviness—these difficulties, trials, and tortures—as light afflictions that last for only a little while. He referred to them as light distress and passing troubles. He viewed them as brief and fleeting. Paul's words encourage us all today that our present troubles are small and won't last long (2 Corinthians 4:17-18). Paul spoke for himself and his companions when he declared, "We're not giving up! We continue to preach! We don't lose heart! Quitting is not an option!"

Difficult situations and difficult people did not harden Paul. In fact, he stated these words with resolve: "We will serve God whether people honor us or despise us. We have great endurance in hardship and in persecutions. We don't lose courage in times of stress and calamity. We remain steadfast and true" (2 Corinthians 6:4b).

Wow. What a statement. Through suffering, Paul continued to serve the Lord. It would have been easier for him to just turn back, but the Lord sustained him. The Lord strengthened him. Paul was being renewed day after day, and his faith continued to excel no matter what. Paul lived a life of great endurance, but he did not simply endure. He lived a life of joy. And it was an abiding joy.

> *Our hearts ache but we always have joy. – 2 Co. 6:10a NLT*
>
> *We are sorrowful but always rejoicing. – AMP*
>
> *We are immersed in tears, yet always filled with deep joy. – MSG*
>
> *We may suffer, yet in every season we are found rejoicing. – TPT*

Paul was experiencing true joy right in the midst of afflictions. How can this be? You see, Paul had learned some things. And we had better learn a thing or two as well. After all, troubles will come. He assured us of that in Second Timothy chapter three and verse twelve when he said, "Anyone who wants to live all out for Christ is in for a lot of trouble; there's no getting around it" (MSG).

Paul had been trained by troubles and had learned some invaluable lessons. He had come to understand that happiness is not circumstantial. Paul did not get stuck in pain or disappointment. He didn't get hung up by his own past failures. He wasn't hindered by his shortcomings or weaknesses; neither did he use them as excuses. In fact, he chose to rejoice in them. He understood that God's power was magnified in his weaknesses. When Paul himself was powerless, God's power was put on display. Above it all, Paul was able to always keep his head about him. He maintained his perspective. The Apostle was not moved by troubles; they mattered little to him. And in Philippians chapter four and verse twelve, Paul said, "I have learned the secret of being content

3

in any and every situation," or as the Message Bible puts it, "I've found the recipe for being happy" (Phil 4:12b MSG).

Dear friend, are you ready to look at some of these secrets? Are you ready to discover some of these ingredients that Paul applied to his life that you, too, might continue to excel even in the midst of the most difficult seasons of your life? Do you want to walk in an abiding joy and happiness no matter what? If so, allow me to share some recipes with you straight from the Word of God!

Guard Clear Thinking with Your Life

Dear friend, guard clear thinking and common sense with your life; don't for a minute lose sight of them. They will keep your soul alive and well.

– Proverbs 3:21-22 MSG

What is your overall state of mind right now? The mind is a powerful thing, and we must learn how to guard it. Our thought life can affect our view of life, and that view can easily become skewed. In fact, the enemy of our soul would like our view of God, His love for us, and the way we process life events to remain skewed. And that, my friend, is exactly why spiritual attacks begin in the mind.

The enemy is always trying to influence our thought life. He wants us to lose our perspective. Often, he does this by throwing up smoke screens so we no longer see clearly. A smoke screen can be those problems and issues that serve to distract and dishearten. According to Oxford Definitions, a smoke screen is described as "a ruse designed to disguise someone's real intentions or activities." Have there been times when you simply did not recognize the enemy's activity in your life? The Bible tells us plainly that our battle is not against flesh and blood but against principalities and spiritual forces of darkness (Eph 6:12). Why do we completely miss this sometimes? Smoke screens! They cause us to lose sight. In military terms, a smoke screen is a cloud of smoke created to conceal military operations. It is something

5

designed to obscure, confuse, or mislead. A smoke screen is something that hides the truth. And there it is in a nutshell: the enemy's smoke screens are intended to hide the truth from us.

The enemy targets and attacks our minds by feeding us lies. The Bible calls Satan a deceiver and the father of lies. His tactics are most often subtle. Before we know it, we will find ourselves coming into agreement and alignment with his lies, believing what he is saying about ourselves, others, and our own circumstances. Proverbs chapter four and verse twenty-three says, "Above all else keep your heart with all diligence, for out of it springs the issues of life."

Keep Your Heart

Alfred Blomfield once made these three statements:

> "On the state of the heart depends the salvation of the soul."

> "From the heart is the fountain or source of life in the sense of happiness."

> "Contentment and happiness in this life depend upon the heart, not upon external circumstances."

Keeping our heads right makes a big impact on our happiness, contentment, and overall well-being. The word "heart" in Proverbs 4:23 is the word *labe* in the original Hebrew language, and it refers to the mind. It is our intellect, our reasoning, our feelings, and our emotional expression. It's the center of everything. The heart, the mind, one's spirit, the soul—it is one's inner life and personhood. It represents a person's innermost thoughts and deepest emotions. It's also the place where our search for God begins and our communion with him takes place. Is it any wonder that these strong instructions from the Word of God begin with these words: "Above all else"? It is critical to get *this* right above everything else. Keep your head right no matter what! It is absolutely vital that we keep or guard our minds and emotions with all diligence. And this must be a continual practice.

The enemy will lie to us and take advantage of situations where we are dealing with any kind of stress. Our stress can offer the enemy an advantage, an opportunity, and a door. We must guard our hearts, especially in times of difficulty and uncertainty. Today, we are living in peculiar times. Understand how the enemy gets in, Friend. The Word of God warns us not to be outwitted by our adversary, the devil. We are not to be ignorant of his devices (2 Co. 2:11). It is time to recognize what lies we have been believing and learn to cast down dangerous, negative thoughts and emotions.

> For though we walk in the flesh, we do not war according to the flesh. For the weapons of our warfare are not carnal but mighty in God for pulling down strongholds, casting down arguments and every high thing that exalts itself against the knowledge of God, bringing every thought into captivity to the obedience of Christ, and being ready to punish all disobedience when your obedience is fulfilled. – 2 Corinthians 10:3-6 NKJV

The Bible refers to these mindsets as arguments and any high thing that raises itself up against the knowledge of God. The King James Version uses the word imaginations. The Passion translation refers to these runaway thoughts as "deceptive fantasies and arrogant attitudes." The Message Bible calls them "warped philosophies and barriers." It also uses the words "loose thoughts and emotions and impulses."

Loose Thoughts and Emotions and Impulses

By your patience possess your souls. – Luke 21:19 NKJV

We must learn to reign in those loose thoughts, and emotions and impulses, and weigh them against the truth of God. The word for "soul" here in Luke 21:19 is the word *psuche* in the original Greek language, and it refers to our mind, spirit, life, and vitality. *Psuche* is referring to the seat of our feelings or emotions, and we are to possess it or keep it by every means possible, especially in the midst of troubles and trials. Dear friend, if you don't possess your soul, someone else will.

> "In your patience possess ye your souls – Be calm and serene, masters of yourselves, and superior to all irrational and disquieting passions. By keeping the government of your spirits, you will both avoid much misery, and guard the better against all dangers." – John Wesley

Do you want to avoid much misery? Rule over your thoughts and emotions! Our minds can be attacked. Our spirits can be broken. Our souls can become downcast. But aren't you glad that they can also be restored, revived, refreshed, transformed, and renewed?

Paul told us in Ephesians chapter four that we must "no longer live as the [unbelieving] Gentiles live, in the futility of their minds," (verse 17) but instead, "continually be renewed in the spirit of your mind [having a fresh, untarnished mental and spiritual attitude]" (verse 23 AMP).

Are you ready to renew your mind? Are you ready to reset your focus?

Today, let's start by removing all smoke screens. Let's begin by recognizing the lies that have attached themselves to our thinking and then remove them, submit them to God, and replace them with His truth. Take some time right now and pray. Ask the Lord to show you any lies you have been believing. I challenge you to write them down and pray over them. Replace every lie with the truth of God found in His Word, and ask the Lord to renew your mind.

Lie: _____ **Truth:** _____

_____ _____

_____ _____

_____ _____

_____ _____

 **PRAYER**

Lord, I submit my thought life to You. I ask You today to reveal any lies that I have been believing about myself, others, and the situations and circumstances in my life. I repent now for coming into agreement with the enemy of my soul. I recognize today that these very things have been compromising my overall happiness, my contentment, and well-being. These things have distracted me and subtracted from me. They have disrupted my peace and disquieted my heart. Reset my focus, Lord. Begin to renew my mind now in Jesus's name.

Be inwardly transformed by the Holy Spirit through a total reformation of how you think. This will empower you to discern God's will as you live a beautiful life, satisfying and perfect in his eyes. – Romans 12:2b TPT

Pull Down Those Strongholds

For the weapons of our warfare are not carnal but mighty in God for pulling down strongholds.

– 2 Corinthians 10:4 NKJV

When you became a Christian, a battle began. It is a battle over your soul and your spirit. And that battle or war always begins with the mind. Therefore, the *fight* must begin right there as well. How do we fight this battle? We begin first by recognizing the lies of the enemy and dealing with them right away before they become strongholds in our lives.

"Strongholds are designed and adapted to oppose the truth and the triumph of the Christian cause." – Albert Barnes

Strongholds are obstacles. They hinder us in every way, and if they remain attached to us long enough, they become strongly fortified places in our lives. Albert Barnes says that this "warfare is to be waged against every strongly fortified place of error and sin. These strong fortifications of error and sin are to be battered down and laid in ruins by our spiritual weapons."

It is imperative that we deal with destructive negative thoughts and emotions created by the lies of the enemy. Second Corinthians chapter ten and verse four tells us that this battle is a spiritual battle and that

God has given us spiritual weapons that are capable and mighty for pulling down strongholds. They cannot stay. They must go!

> *For though we walk in the flesh, we do not war according to the flesh. For the weapons of our warfare are not carnal but mighty in God for pulling down strongholds, casting down arguments and every high thing that exalts itself against the knowledge of God, bringing every thought into captivity to the obedience of Christ, and being ready to punish all disobedience when your obedience is fulfilled. – 2 Corinthians 10:4-6 NKJV*

Our spiritual weapons are sufficient for destroying strongholds. Our weapons are completely capable of demolishing these mindsets. Let's bring down these barriers that have been hindering us from experiencing true, lasting happiness. After recounting a few ups and downs and twists and turns of his life, Paul makes this declaration:

> *I can do all things through Christ who strengthens me. – Philippians 4:13 NKJV*

This little word "do" in verse thirteen translates like this: "to exercise force and to prevail." We have to put some action to some things, and we can begin right here by literally getting ahold of our thought life. It's time to guard our minds against what I refer to as irrational thoughts and feelings. We must recognize the lies we have been believing about ourselves, others, and the situations that we walk through. We must learn to confront the lies with the truth of God, and we must be very intentional and matter-of-fact about this. The term "cast down" in Second Corinthians 10:5 translates as "to lower with violence." The Passion Translation uses the words "capture like a prisoner of war." These are very aggressive terms. There is nothing passive about it! This does not equate to just sitting back and accepting everything that comes our way. We take action.

How do we fight this battle for the mind and maintain the victory? The rest of the passage gives us the answer. We cast down those thoughts that raise themselves up against the knowledge of God (NKJV). We demolish deceptive fantasies that oppose Him. We break through every arrogant attitude that falsely believes that it knows better than God does (TPT). We smash warped philosophies and tear down barriers that the enemy has erected against God's truth (MSG). That's what the Word of God instructs us to do! This is the battle plan and operational mission straight from the Lord of Hosts.

Cast down, smash, tear down, demolish, break through—these are some pretty strong words. The Passion Translation puts it like this:

> We capture, like prisoners of war, every thought and insist that it bow in obedience to the Anointed One. – 2 Corinthians 10:5b TPT

This creates a strong image for us, doesn't it? We are going to have to get engaged in this battle and take back control of our own thought life, our own peace of mind, and our own lives. And sometimes that means letting the enemy know in no uncertain terms that he will not influence, manipulate, or control our lives in any way, shape, or form. We must begin now by ruling or governing our own thought life. Let's become more disciplined than we've ever been before!

> The world is unprincipled. It's dog-eat-dog out there! The world doesn't fight fair. But we don't live or fight our battles that way – never have and never will. The tools of our trade aren't for marketing or manipulation, but they are for demolishing that entire massively corrupt culture. We use our powerful God-tools for smashing warped philosophies, tearing down barriers erected against the truth of God, fitting every loose thought and emotion and impulse into the structure of life shaped by Christ. Our tools are ready at hand for clearing the ground of every obstruction and building lives of obedience into maturity. – 2 Corinthians 10:3-6 MSG

Let's be honest. It *is* a mean world, and we are dealing with difficult things and difficult people all the time, but we cannot allow what is happening on the outside to get inside. We've got to keep our heads no matter what. Today, we put a stop to irrational thoughts and emotions, and we no longer make room for them.

Paul gives us a recipe for guarding our hearts and minds in Philippians chapter four.

> *Be anxious for nothing, but in everything by prayer and supplication, with thanksgiving, let your requests be made known to God; and the peace of God, which surpasses all understanding, will guard your hearts and minds through Christ Jesus. – Philippians 4:6-7 NKJV*

In times when anxiety wants to settle in, pray. Then with thanksgiving, present your requests before the Lord. And meditate on these things:

> *Finally, brethren, whatever things are true, whatever things are noble, whatever things are just, whatever things are pure, whatever things are lovely, whatever things are of good report, if there is any virtue and if there is anything praiseworthy—meditate on these things. – Philippians 4:8 NKJV*

Notice that the very first thing we are to meditate on is truth. What has been consuming your mind? What have you been dwelling on and filling your thoughts with? What kind of things have you been meditating on?

Train yourself to reject the lies of the enemy and cast down destructive negative thoughts and emotions daily. Make it a habit.

> *But solid food is for the mature, for those who have their powers of discernment trained by constant practice to distinguish good from evil. – Hebrews 5:14 ESV*

What are you practicing in order to become more discerning? What habits are you forming to sharpen your ability to quickly recognize good from evil, truth from lies?

"Purify, then, and elevate the heart, keep it above all keeping, as a tender plant to be nursed and guarded in an unkindly soil."
– Alfred Blomfield

 **PRAYER**

Lord, right now in the name of Jesus, I cast down every lie of the enemy. I take authority over every thought and discern whether it is coming straight from the pit of Hell. I tear down wrong thinking and replace it with God's truth. I will govern my own thoughts, emotions, and impulses. I will guard my heart against warped philosophies. I will have nothing to do with deceptive fantasies. I refuse to have an arrogant attitude. I will consciously and purposely fix my thoughts on the things of God. May every stronghold in my life be pulled down. Help me to break destructive habits and form good and right habits in Jesus's name.

"Whatever we plant in our subconscious mind and nourish with repetition and emotion will one day become a reality."
– Earl Nightingale

Fresh Perspective

You will keep in perfect and constant peace the one whose mind is steadfast [that is, committed and focused on You – in both inclination and character].
– Isaiah 26:3a AMP

A renewed mind and fresh perspective can bring about glorious change! Have you been thinking clearly lately? Are you taking charge of your thought life? Are you fixing your focus on the right things? Isaiah 26:3 speaks of a steadfast mind. The word for mind that is used in this text refers to "imaginations that form and frame one's reality." A steadfast mind is one that is steady and unwavering. A steadfast mind is an important thing. Whatever we fix our mind upon can greatly affect the quality of our life.

"If the thoughts are ordered well, the outward life will follow."
– *The Pulpit Commentary*

If anyone in the New Testament had a steadfast mind, it was Paul. I love that no matter what was going on in Paul's life, no matter how difficult or intense the circumstances were around him, he did not lose his perspective! Paul had a way of looking at what was going right rather than only seeing what was going wrong. This is evident in scriptures like these:

We are hard pressed on every side, yet not crushed; we are perplexed, but not in despair; persecuted, but not forsaken; struck down, but not destroyed. – 2 Corinthians 4:8-9 NKJV

Even though our outward man is perishing, yet the inward man is being renewed day by day. – 2 Corinthians 4:16b NKJV

Paul was not focusing on the difficulties. In fact, he viewed them as only temporary, and he weighed them against eternity.

For our light affliction, which is for a moment, is working for us a far more exceeding and eternal weight of glory. – 2 Corinthians 4:17 NKJV

On top of being able to look at things long-term, Paul considered his present trials as light afflictions. My goodness! If Paul considered his afflictions as light, how should we be considering ours? And what about his infirmities, his weaknesses, and limitations? Did he allow them to stop him or bring him down? Second Corinthians chapter twelve mentions the thorn in Paul's flesh that he struggled with. Paul said that he had begged the Lord three times to take it from him, but the Lord did *not* heal him of this condition. Instead, God told Paul that His grace was sufficient for him. Nowhere in Scripture do we see Paul becoming angry with God for not answering this request the way he wanted him to. Paul never felt that God owed him one single thing for living his life in complete abandonment for the Gospel. Instead, Paul took the Lord's words to heart as God told him that His grace was all that he needed and that His power worked best in weakness. In fact, Paul stopped focusing on his handicap and began looking at the condition as a gift—something to boast about and rejoice over.

Once I heard that, I was glad to have it happen. I quit focusing on the handicap and began appreciating the gift. It was a case of Christ's strength moving in on my weakness. Now I take limitations in stride, and with good cheer, these limitations that cut me down to size – abuse, accidents, opposition, bad breaks. I just let Christ take over! And so the weaker I get, the stronger I become. – 2 Corinthians 12:9-10 MSG

So I will celebrate my weakness. – 2 Corinthians 12:9b TPT

I am not defeated by my weakness, but delighted. – 2 Corinthians 12:10a TPT

How was Paul able to maintain such optimism? One of the keys to his being able to keep this kind of life perspective is found directly in Second Corinthians chapter four and verse eighteen. After remarking that he and his ministry companions had dealt with trouble after trouble, Paul made this statement:

So we don't look at the troubles we can see now; rather, we fix our gaze on things that cannot be seen. For the things we see now will soon be gone, but the things we cannot see will last forever. – 2 Corinthians 4:18 NLT

Paul said that he was not looking at all the problems. He wasn't focusing on those things. He wasn't giving his attention to the trouble or dwelling on the circumstances. Imagine how defeated, depressed, and forgotten he might have felt if he had. It would have exhausted him and sucked the very life right out of him.

How about you and me today? Are we focusing only on what's wrong rather than what's right? Do we dwell only on the problem itself? Are we, as they say, looking at the glass as half empty rather than half full?

*Summing it all up, friends, I'd say you'll do best by filling your minds and meditating on things true, noble, reputable, authentic, compelling, gracious – **the best, not the worst; the beautiful, not the ugly; things to praise, not things to curse.** – Philippians 4:8 MSG (Emphasis added)*

Paul was able to keep his perspective even in the midst of everything falling apart around him. He was not grumbling or complaining, but seemed hopeful, reenergized, and all the more determined. There is quite a difference between a positive, hopeful person and a negative, complaining person. Look at what Alfred Blomfield had to say about this very thing:

> "Observe the difference between the man who is blessed with a cheerful and hopeful heart, and the one who has a desponding and complaining heart—not the heart-sickness only which comes of hope deferred, but the heart-jaundice which turns hope itself into despair. While the cheerful heart can find happiness even under circumstances the most depressing, the complaining heart will turn even the most encouraging into misery.

> "Look at the despondence of happiness on tenderness and kindness of heart. Is it too much to say that the man of hard and cruel heart is in the end far more cruel to himself than he can be to anyone else? In himself he tears out by the roots the plant of happiness and dries up at its very springs the 'fountain of life.'"

Paul wasn't denying that there were difficulties. He just wasn't consumed with the difficulties. Like us, Paul was just a person with a human nature, frailties, imperfections, and weaknesses. Paul was an emotional being with human feelings, but he wasn't ruled by them. Paul centered his mind on the things of God, and the Word of God was implanted in his heart. He was a man who walked in the Spirit and not in the flesh, and he urged us to do the same.

If we live in the Spirit, let us also walk in the Spirit. – Galatians 5:25 NKJV

Walking in the Spirit is about being under the influence of the Holy Spirit and living by faith. When we walk in the Spirit, we walk according to the rule of His holy Word. We are not under the world's influence or direction. And our human emotions are not our guide. You see, Paul wasn't just taking a positive approach to life. He was walking in the Spirit. He was living by faith and not by his sight.

For we walk by faith, not by sight. – 2 Corinthians 5:7 NKJV

The apostle Paul wasn't relying on the things that he was able to see with his natural eyes. Paul had the ability to see with spiritual eyes. Our perspective is our sight. It's the ability to see things in a true relationship. And what we see around us in the natural realm is not always revealing the truth. Things aren't always the way they appear. Paul understood this.

> *There's far more here than meets the eye. The things we see now are here today, gone tomorrow. But the things we can't see now will last forever. – 2 Corinthians 4:18 MSG*

Like Paul, we must develop the ability to see with spiritual eyes, so we are never shaken by what we see in the natural realm. We can no longer be swayed by what we see with our physical eyes. We must be able to see with the eyes of the Spirit from the position of knowing His Word and living by our faith. Faith is not limited to physical sight. Faith gives us a new set of eyes, new vision, and a new perspective. We must develop spiritual sight. Where do we get this spiritual sight? Jesus said to come to Him. He is our source and will become to us the "eye salve."

> *Purchase eye salve to be placed over your eyes so that you can truly see. All those I dearly love I unmask and train. – Revelations 3:18b-19a TPT*

> *The precepts of the Lord are right, rejoicing the heart; the commandment of the Lord is pure, enlightening the eyes. – Psalm 19:8 NKJV*

We get this spiritual sight straight from the Spirit of the Lord through His Word. Spiritual sight comes directly from Him.

We look away from the natural realm and we fasten our gaze onto Jesus who birthed faith within us and who leads us forward into faith's perfection. – Hebrews 12:2a TPT

PRAYER

Lord, give me a steadfast mind and eyes of the Spirit. Train me so I can truly see! Continue to remove the blinders from my eyes. Give me good spiritual vision! Develop a cheerful and hopeful heart within me— one that can find happiness under any and all circumstances. Help me to walk in the Spirit and by faith. Today, I fix my focus wholly on You. I will deliberately direct my thoughts toward what is true, noble, reputable, authentic, compelling, and gracious. Order my thoughts as well as my steps, Lord! In Jesus's name.

Yes, feast on all the treasures of the heavenly realm and fill your thoughts with heavenly realities, and not with the distractions of the natural realm. – Colossians 3:2-3 TPT

Day 4

A Contented Mind is a Continual Feast

I have learned in whatever state I am, to be content
– Philippians 4:11 NKJV

Contentment is a condition of the heart. It's a state of mind. Paul said that he knew how to be content in all situations and that it was something he had learned to do. Some of us have been waiting for everything to fall into place first. When everything works out right, then we will be happy. When God answers that prayer, then we'll be content. When we get that job promotion, then we'll be satisfied. And on and on it goes. Is contentment based on specific outward conditions? The Word of God doesn't indicate that it is, and here in Philippians chapter four, we see Paul's life example. He tells us that the personal, inward contentment that he enjoyed was learned.

I love the way R.M. Edgar describes contentment, especially as related to this Scripture. He says that contentment is an art! It's something that must be learned!

> "We cannot acquire it at a bound. We must serve our apprenticeship to it as to any other art. It is not a science to be theoretically mastered, but an art to be practically obtained. We must go to the 'school of art,' we must set ourselves earnestly as

scholars to learn the lesson, and we must 'keep our hands in' by constant practice."

Paul had learned many invaluable lessons, and one of those lessons was how to be content no matter the circumstances.

For I have learned how to be content (satisfied to the point where I am not disturbed or disquieted) in whatever state I am. – Philippians 4:11 AMPC

The *Jamieson, Fausset, and Brown's Commentary on the Whole Bible* says that the word "I" here in Philippians 4:11 in the Greek language is emphatical and that verse eleven can be interpreted much like this, "I leave it to others, if they will, to be discontented. I, for my part, have learned, by the teaching of the Holy Spirit, and the dealings of Providence, to be content in every state."

It sounds to me like Paul made a decision about it. It's really up to me and you to take what we have learned and apply it to our lives, or we can continue repeating negative cycles. Let's get off the merry-go-round so we can begin living our best life now. First Timothy tells us that godliness with contentment is great gain.

Now godliness with contentment is great gain. – 1 Timothy 6:6 KJV

The word "contentment" here refers to "a state of mind; a calm and satisfied feeling; a freedom from murmuring and complaining." Guarding your thought life, ruling your own soul, casting down thoughts that are from the pit of hell, demolishing destructive mindsets, regaining the right perspective, and being able to see with spiritual eyes rather than natural eyes—these are essential ingredients for contentment. The outward conditions should not be ruling the state of the heart, but the state of the heart should be governing outward conditions. What is the condition of your heart today?

There is an old saying that goes something like this: "A contented mind is a continual feast." Is this scriptural? It certainly is and it's found in Proverbs 15:15.

All the days of the afflicted are evil, but he who is of a merry heart has a continual feast. – Proverbs 15:15 NKJV

Let's take a closer look at this Scripture. The "afflicted" person that the first part of the verse is referring to translates more closely toward a troubled and downcast spirit than it does toward outward conditions like poverty, pain, or sickness. *Ellicott's Commentary for the English Reader* gives this interpretation:

"The 'afflicted' here evidently means, not one who has to bear great misfortunes, but one who makes the worst of everything, to whom the 'clouds return after the rain;' while the one who is 'of merry heart' does just the contrary."

And *The Pulpit Commentary* puts it like this:

"The persons intended are such as take a gloomy view of things; who are always in low spirits, and cannot rise superior to present circumstances. These never have a happy moment; they are always taking anxious thoughts, and forecasting evil."

Perhaps the Amplified Classic Version of Proverbs 15:15 brings forth the best translation for us today.

All the days of the desponding and afflicted are made evil [by anxious thought and forebodings], but he who has a glad heart has a continual feast [regardless of circumstances]. – Proverbs 15:15 AMPC

What we are really contrasting here are two different conditions of the heart: the despondent, anxious heart and the glad, contented heart. Once again, we see this Hebrew word *labe* used for the word "heart" in this particular Scripture. It refers to the mind, will, inner man, understanding, soul, the seat of our emotions, and even the seat of our courage. We can see, then, how important a steadfast, glad mind really is. This contented mind is compared to the cheerfulness of a feast. This feast is relating to a constant satisfaction and delight in our hearts. It is a fixed state of joy and contentment.

Paul knew how to abound and how to be in lack. When he was abounding, he was content. When he was in lack, he was content. He was at peace and was happy because of his relationship with God and the confident trust he had in God. Paul had learned to be content. He made a decision, and because of it, he was able to say these words:

> I can do all things [which He has called me to do] through Him who strengthens and empowers me [to fulfill His purpose – I am self-sufficient in Christ's sufficiency; I am ready for anything and equal to anything through Him who infuses me with inner strength and confident peace.] – Philippians 4:13 AMP

Paul had been trained and prepared well by the very experiences of his life that the Lord had allowed him to endure. God continually filled and refilled Paul with His power. He received inner strength from on high. Paul could do anything through Christ. His confidence was in God and not himself. He was ready for anything!

It is time for us to be infused with inner strength fresh and anew. It's time for us to feast on the goodness of God. It's time for us to know and enjoy this happy heart, this perpetual feast, this continual festival of contentment and joy. I believe that we can have the best of God even in the worst of times. Are you ready to be infused with new strength fresh and anew?

> A cheerful heart is good medicine, but a broken spirit saps a person's strength. – Proverbs 17:22 NLT

 **PRAYER**

Help me to break any cycles of negativity in my life and master this art of being content in all circumstances. Deliver me, oh Lord, from anxious thoughts and forebodings. Give me a steady heart and a sound mind. Today, I choose to be glad. May I partake of this feast from the Lord. May I be filled and satisfied, always. And may the joy of the Lord be my strength.

Your spiritual roots go deeply into his life as you are continually infused with strength, encouraged in every way. For you are established in the faith you have absorbed and enriched by your devotion to him! – Colossians 2:7 TPT

Count It All Joy

*My brethren, count it all joy when you fall into various difficulties, knowing
that the testing of your faith produces patience. But let patience have its
perfect work, that you may be perfect and complete, lacking nothing.*

– James 1:2-4 NKJV

Now that's perspective! James chapter one tells us to count it ALL
joy! The trials, the difficulties, the testing of our faith—begin to look
at these things with a fresh set of eyes. We may not be happy about
the circumstances themselves, but we can be glad and rejoice over
the valuable virtues that will be developed within us as we continue
to stand. Nothing is wasted in the kingdom of God! Good things are
being produced on the inside. Let trials make you better and not bitter.
It's God's desire to use difficulties in a way that benefits you. Patience
is being developed. Growth and maturity are taking place as you press
on through. God is pouring into you the very things that you have
been lacking in your character. Troubles may seem to be subtracting
something from you, but the reality is that God is adding something to
you through the experience of these difficulties, things that may not
otherwise be acquired. We come out of our trials possessing something
that we didn't have before the entire experience. We find that we have
gained some wisdom. We have gained some intestinal fortitude. New
and unseen things have been released to us. The Passion Translation
encourages us to look at these times as opportunities to experience the
greatest joy we can!

My fellow believers, when it seems as though you are facing nothing but difficulties, see it as an invaluable opportunity to experience the greatest joy that you can! For you know that when your faith is tested it stirs up power within you to endure all things. And then as your endurance grows even stronger it will release perfection into every part of your being until there is nothing missing and nothing lacking. – James 1:2-4 TPT

Nothing missing and nothing lacking; I like that! The subtitle listed for this passage of Scripture in the Passion Translation reads, "Profiting from Trials." Truly, we are being blessed in the midst of our struggles. We just don't always see it that way. The Amplified version tells us that we should "consider it nothing but joy." Don't look at it any other way! Begin to thank God for what He is going to produce and deposit in you through every difficulty. The truth of God's Word says that you are blessed!

If your faith remains strong, even while surrounded by life's difficulties, you will continue to experience the untold blessings of God! True happiness comes as you pass the test with faith, and receive the victorious crown of life promised to every lover of God! – James 1:12 TPT

Don't fret when you face trials and your faith feels like it's being tested. There is a greater gift and reward being released to you. Open your spiritual eyes and see it! The first chapter of the book of James tells us that every good and perfect gift comes from the Lord (verse 17). But wait! Verse two tells us to consider even the tests and challenges of our lives as gifts.

Consider it a sheer gift, friend, when tests and challenges come at you from all sides. You know that under pressure, your faith-life is forced into the open and shows its true colors. So don't try to get out of anything prematurely. Let it do its work so you become mature and well-developed, not deficient in any way. – James 1: 2-4 MSG

Trials, difficulties, tests, challenges, and pressures can be considered gifts. After all, they come with many rewards. If we can keep this truth in mind, we can face difficulties head on and trust the Lord while we do it. Like Paul, we will find ourselves declaring that we, too, can do all things through Christ who strengthens us. James chapter one and verse twelve lets us know that there is light at the end of the tunnel, so let's develop some good tunnel vision. Keep your eye on the prize.

> *Anyone who meets a testing challenge head-on and manages to stick it out is mighty fortunate. For such a person loyally in love with God, the reward is life and more life. — James 1:12 MSG*

Life and more life. We're talking about abundant life now and eternal life hereafter. And we begin to access it through both hearing and applying the principles found in God's Word. We must respond to His truths and walk in them. Verse twenty-two tells us that we must be doers of the word and not merely hearers. Otherwise, we deceive ourselves.

> *But be doers of the word, and not hearers only, deceiving yourselves. — James 1:22 NKJV*

We have an enemy, Satan, who loves to deceive us, but it's also important to note that if we merely hear the Word of God and never apply it, we are deceiving ourselves. Don't lie to yourself, Friend. God's principles work. His Word is still for today. It's alive and active. It's sharper than any two-edged sword. We can stand on the Word of God.

> *But he who looks into the perfect law of liberty and continues in it, and is not a forgetful hearer but a doer of the word, this one will be blessed in what he does. — James 1:25 NKJV*

The word "blessed" in this verse is the word *makarios* in the original Greek language, and it translates as happy! Blessed, fortunate, and happy—that's who you are according to God. Reset your perspective today. Look away from the issues and problems and fix your eyes on Jesus, the author and finisher of your faith. Gaze deeply into the perfecting law of liberty, which is His infallible Word. Respond to the truth and be strengthened by it. It has the power to continually deliver you. Consistently apply it to your life, not only when it's easy but even when it's hard. Run swiftly to the Word; cling to it and crave it with every fiber of your being. His Word is truth. His Word is strength. His Word is our very sustenance.

The revelation of God is whole and pulls our lives together. The signposts of God are clear and point out the right road. The life-maps of God are right, showing the way to joy. – Psalm 19:7-8 MSG

PRAYER

Lord, change my perspective where tests and trials are concerned. Help me to count it *all* joy and to experience the greatest joy that I can even in the midst of difficulties. Work in the very areas of my heart where I have been lacking in my character. Strengthen me. Make me whole and complete until I am lacking nothing! Stir up Your power within me. Thank you, Lord, that I am becoming a person of great endurance. I will hold fast to Your Word. I will trust in You!

Oh, how I love all you've revealed; I reverently ponder it all day long. Your commands give me an edge on my enemies, they never become obsolete. – Psalm 119:97-98 MSG

Prepare the Soil

We use our powerful God-tools for smashing warped philosophies, tearing down barriers erected against the truth of God, fitting every loose thought and emotion and impulse into the structure of life shaped by Christ. Our tools are ready at hand for clearing the ground of every obstruction and building lives of obedience into maturity.

– 2 Corinthians 10:4-6 MSG

At some point in time in our lives, every one of us has been affected negatively by events that have taken place. There comes a time when we have to regain clear thinking and realign our hearts. We must train our eyes and spirit not to be influenced by what we hear and see taking place around us but what we know is true from the inerrant Word of God. We put our God tools to work, and we do it because we absolutely want lives shaped by Christ. We want to experience that abundant life that Christ came to give us. We want the peace of God, the exceedingly great joy of the Lord, happiness, and contentment. That life belongs to us as children of God. But make no mistake about it: A life shaped by Christ is not a life exempt from difficulties and trials. God never promised us a smooth, carefree, easy way. That's simply not biblical. He did, however, promise that He would take the difficulties that we face and use them for our benefit. And He promised that He would be with us in the fire. He will even take what the enemy of our soul meant for harm and use it for our good. In God's good purposes, He will use hardships to mature us and to make us complete.

Although there may be battles, He will cause us to become more than conquerors and super victorious. We will become well trained and prepared by difficulties. God will continually empower us and fill us with fresh strength. We must partner with Him in these things. So, we pick up our God tools and we begin clearing the ground of any and every obstruction. We prepare the soil of our hearts to receive God's best.

Obstructions

What has been hindering and blocking your overall mental and emotional health, your happiness and general well-being? What has been sabotaging your spiritual growth? Ask the Lord right now to show you if there is anything needing to be cleared away once and for all. It's God's desire, as we will see in the following days, that we flourish and thrive in every season of our lives. Let's do some soul searching and digging today.

In simple humility, let our gardener, God, landscape you with the Word, making a salvation-garden of your life. – James 1:21 MSG

James 1:21 paints a beautiful picture for us. A salvation garden. What a thought to meditate upon and pray over. Oh, Lord, landscape me with Your Word! Come and till the soil of my heart and make a beautiful salvation garden of my life.

In the natural, we know a few things about landscaping and growing a garden, don't we? Clearing the ground, cultivating, and tilling must first take place. Clearing the ground is not an easy task. And in order to get the job done, it's important to have the right tools and equipment ready at hand. Land clearing is a process of removing objects that are prohibiting the land from being of good use. It involves removing overgrown brush, unwanted vegetation, and tree stumps. Old roots and root systems need to be dug up and cleared away. The removal of rocks and other obstructions from the soil is necessary. The landscaper will look over the land and decide what to keep and what to get rid of. He will test the soil to determine whether it is suitable for what he is wanting to plant.

Once the land has been cleared, it is ready to be cultivated. This is the process of breaking up and loosening the soil. Nature takes its toll on the soil, and it becomes hard and dry. The soil can become compacted by rain and other things like regular foot traffic. Cultivation breaks up the hardened soil. Loosening the soil and removing the weeds are vital for many reasons. The breaking up of the soil allows air, water, and nutrients to be able to penetrate the soil where plant roots can gain access to them. Weeds will only compete for the water and nutrients, so they must be removed for the garden to really thrive. This loosening of the soil also makes it easier for the newly germinated seeds to sprout through the surface of the soil when it's time.

Cultivating and tilling are done before you lay down the seed. In gardening, tilling is very similar to cultivating. Tilling, however, is more intensive. It's more thorough. The idea is to go deeper and turn up more soil. The roots of new plants can then grow deeper and spread out, and microorganisms for plant growth have a much better environment to thrive in. Tilling is usually done when preparing the soil for a new garden, but it is also done at the end of each growing season.

Now let's take a closer look at James 1:21. The passage begins by instructing us to get rid of the things in our hearts that do not please the Lord.

> Post this at all the intersections, dear friends: Lead with your ears, follow up with your tongue, and let anger straggle along in the rear. God's righteousness doesn't grow from human anger. So throw all spoiled virtue and cancerous evil in the garbage. In simple humility, let our gardener, God, landscape you with the Word, making a salvation-garden of your life. – James 1:19-21 MSG

Evil speech and anger are just a few things pinpointed here. The New King James Version puts it like this:

Therefore lay aside all filthiness and overflow of wickedness, and receive with meekness the implanted word, which is able to save your souls. – James 1:21 NKJV

We must get rid of any form of sin in our hearts and break through the places that have become hardened. Is there anything within the soil of your heart that you need to lay aside, abandon, do away with, or, simply put, get rid of? Are there any hard places in your heart? If so, what has caused your heart to become hardened?

We cannot allow the events of our lives—past, present, or future—to cause our hearts to become hardened. It is time to let those things go. Let's rid ourselves of anything that does not please the Lord and begin to allow the Word of God to be implanted and rooted in our hearts without one single hindrance.

Let your roots grow down into him, and let your lives be built on him. – Colossians 2:7a NLT

PRAYER

Lord Jesus, I come before you in simple humility today. Show me if there is anything in my own heart that may be hindering me from receiving all that You have for me. Put Your finger on anything in my heart that doesn't please You. Bring it to my immediate attention that I might rid myself of everything that has been blocking my blessing. Break up any hardened areas within me and heal me through and through. Uproot any old root systems that are not from You. Landscape my life and make it what You desire it to be. Fill me. Empower me. I desire to have a life shaped by Christ! I desire to grow and thrive!

Plow up the hard ground of your hearts! Do not waste your good seed among thorns. – Jeremiah 4:3 NLT

Receive the Good Seed

Consider this: There was a farmer who went out to sow seeds.
– Matthew 13:3 TPT

In James chapter one and verse twenty-one, God is our gardener. He desires that we grow, flourish, and thrive. And here in the Parable of the Sower, God is the farmer, and He is sowing good seed. The seed being sown is the Word of God. It is the incorruptible seed. This seed is imperishable. It will not decay. All the life and the potential are contained within the seed. Oh, how important it is for us to receive this seed!

> *For you have been born again, not of perishable seed, but of imperishable, through the living and enduring word of God.*
> *– 1 Peter 1:23 NIV*

Whether we have realized it or not, our very salvation was dependent upon the seed. Albert Barnes says that we were born again "by truth, communicating a living principle to the soul which can never decay." He goes on to say that "divine truth is made the instrument of quickening the soul into spiritual life." Without the seed of God's Word heard, understood, and quickened within our hearts, we could not even be born again! In the Parable of the Sower, Jesus addresses four different types of soil, referring to the condition of the heart of man. The growth of the seed is dependent upon the condition of the

37

soil. And here in this parable, Jesus focuses our attention upon the obstacles the seed encounters. Let's look at these hindrances and consider some things.

> *That same day Jesus went out of the house and sat by the lake. Such large crowds gathered around him that he got into a boat and sat in it, while all the people stood on the shore. Then he told them many things in parables, saying: "A farmer went out to sow his seed. As he was scattering the seed, some fell along the path, and the birds came and ate it up. Some fell on rocky places, where it did not have much soil. It sprang up quickly, because the soil was shallow. But when the sun came up, the plants were scorched, and they withered because they had no root. Other seed fell among thorns, which grew up and choked the plants. Still other seed fell on good soil, where it produced a crop—a hundred, sixty or thirty times what was sown. Whoever has ears, let them hear.*
>
> *"Listen then to what the parable of the sower means: When anyone hears the message about the kingdom and does not understand it, the evil one comes and snatches away what was sown in their heart. This is the seed sown along the path. The seed falling on rocky ground refers to someone who hears the word and at once receives it with joy. But since they have no root, they last only a short time. When trouble or persecution comes because of the word, they quickly fall away. The seed falling among the thorns refers to someone who hears the word, but the worries of this life and the deceitfulness of wealth choke the word, making it unfruitful. But the seed falling on good soil refers to someone who hears the word and understands it. This is the one who produces a crop, yielding a hundred, sixty or thirty times what was sown." – Matthew 13:3-9, 18-23 NIV*

Jesus spoke of four different types of soil, all marked by certain characteristics. The first type of soil is referred to as soil that was along the path. This soil has not yet been plowed. It is the hard, dry soil that has been trodden down. The seed cannot penetrate the surface of the soil; therefore, the birds come, snatch up the seed, and carry it away. The condition of this beaten path seems to be one of neglect. The condition being addressed refers to the person who actually hears the Word but does not understand it or may not recognize their need. The Word simply has not penetrated their heart and the enemy is quick to steal that word and make it of no effect.

The second type of soil is referred to as rocky places. This soil is shallow with rock or hard places directly underneath. The seed was able to enter the little bit of loose soil at the surface and quickly sprout. However, there was no depth, and the seed found no place to take root. Therefore, the plant was unable to receive sufficient nutrients and water to nourish it. Consequently, the plant withered in the heat of the sun just as quickly as it had sprouted. It shriveled up as a result of an insufficient root system. The condition being addressed here refers to the person who hears the Word and gladly receives it yet does not profit from it. The heart is not changed by the Word. And when temptation, trials, or troubles come, this person falls away. The difficulties become a stumbling block to them. This is a sad state, really, because so much potential existed. Matthew Henry says that "many endure for a while, that do not endure to the end, and so come short of the happiness which is promised to them only that persevere (Matthew 10:22); they did run well, but something hindered them (Gal. 5:7)."

The next type of soil spoken of is full of thorns. The seed was scattered among these thorns. Then the thorns grew up with the plant and choked it. This soil represents soil that has not been thoroughly cleared. Those thorns, the overbrush, shrubs, and weeds crowd out any good growth. And the condition of the person being referred to here is one who is overcome with the cares of this world. They have received the Word and even developed a root system, but stress, worry, and fear creep in much like the thorns. These things suffocate their faith and become such a hindrance to a flourishing, thriving life. The verse speaks specifically about the deceitfulness of wealth as well. It's not wealth itself but the deceitfulness of it. It is when we put our confidence, trust, and security in wealth rather than the Lord that it becomes a snare. It's when the material things are first place in our hearts that they become an obstacle. The deception is that worldly things bring true, lasting happiness and fulfillment. The truth is they do not. Being preoccupied with the cares of this life will certainly become a hindrance. The heart of the believer in this example received the good seed, but it became unfruitful.

"The stones spoiled the root, the thorns spoil the fruit."
– Matthew Henry

And finally, the fourth type of soil is good soil. This soil had been plowed, cleared, and prepared. It was free from any hindrances. The seed entered the soil and took root. Those roots went deep and spread out. The plants were then able to receive all the nutrients they needed. They were able to spring up and bring forth fruit. There was no loss! The Word of God was heard, understood, and quickened within the heart. Growth continued to take place and a good harvest was enjoyed.

Where do you find yourself in this parable? Take some time today and pray over this. It is time for our hearts to be free and clear—no obstructions!

But other seeds fell on good, rich soil that kept producing a good harvest. Some yielded thirty, some sixty, and some even one hundred times as much as he planted! If you're able to understand this, then you need to respond. – Matthew 13:8-9 TPT

 **PRAYER**

Thank you, Lord, for Your Word. May it always penetrate my heart and accomplish just what You intend for it to accomplish in my life. Allow my life to be changed by it. I will not neglect the reading of Your Word, but I will receive it and allow You to tend the soil of my heart. Break up the rocky ground of my heart! Remove the weeds and the thorns! Help me to always recognize my need and yield to Your Holy Spirit. I receive Your Word today. May it enter my heart and go deep. And may Your Word take root and spread out wide. Give me a steady heart, free from the cares of this world. I will trust You, Lord. Bring forth a good harvest in and through me in Jesus's name.

The seed cast on good earth is the person who hears and takes in
the News, and then produces a harvest beyond his wildest dreams.
– Matthew 13:23 MSG

Springing Up with New Life

Give ear, O heavens, and I will speak; and hear, O earth, the words of my mouth. Let my teaching drop as the rain, My speech distill as the dew, as raindrops on the tender herb, and as showers on the grass.

– Deuteronomy 32:1-2 NKJV

Our hearts say, "Yes, Lord, we will listen and receive every Word you speak to our hearts!"

When we receive the Word of God into our hearts and spirits, we will begin to grow and flourish. His Word is the seed, and as we continue to receive His teachings and precepts, they become as the rain, refreshing us, filling us, and providing all that we need in our inner being. Without the rain, nature will become dry and barren. Without His Word, so will the believer.

> *Just as the rain and snow descend from the skies and don't go back until they've watered the earth, doing their work of making things grow and blossom, producing seed for farmers and food for the hungry, so will the words that come out of my mouth not come back empty handed.* – Isaiah 55:10-11 MSG

We find such a powerful analogy in Isaiah chapter fifty-five verses ten and eleven. Rain and snow soak into the ground. As their waters reach the seed that has been sown, it causes it to sprout and spring up with new life! This natural rain and snow are sent from heaven to accomplish a great purpose—His purpose. Likewise, God said that His Word will not return to Him without accomplishing what He intends. His Word is powerful, alive, and active. Just imagine what He might bring forth from the soil of the human heart that has been implanted with His Word. His Word planted in the heart produces a good harvest. It nourishes us and sustains us. It is food for the human soul, and we are to crave it.

> *Like newborn babies, you must crave pure spiritual milk so that you will grow into a full experience of salvation. Cry out for this nourishment, now that you have had a taste of the Lord's kindness.*
> *— 1 Peter 2:2-3 NLT*

This "pure spiritual milk" in 1 Peter 2:1-3 is the sustaining power of God's Word. It nourishes and strengthens our inner being. In this Scripture, the term "milk" is not referring to elementary truths as it is in 1 Corinthians 3:2 or Hebrews 5:12-13. Here it is emphasizing spiritual nourishment that is absolutely vital for our growth. We are to hunger and thirst for His Word much in the same way that a nursing baby cries out for its mother's breast milk. The word for "babies" in this text in the original language describes a baby at the breast, one who is dependent upon the mother's milk for nourishment. Newborn babies drink frequently and regularly. They express their hunger by impatiently crying out until they are full, satisfied, and soothed. What is being implied here is that you and I are to crave, desire, long for, and yearn for His Word with intensity. There is no spiritual growth apart from the intake of this pure spiritual milk.

Billy Graham once said, "Just as our bodies need food, so our souls need spiritual food. Without it, we become malnourished and weak, susceptible to every temptation and unable to do the work God calls us to do." You see, this nourishment is not just for the brand-new Christian. It is for all believers' continued growth, maturity, strength, direction, well-being, success, blessing, and effectiveness. His Word reveals Christ and increases our love for Him. Through His Word, we come to know Him better, and we become increasingly more like Him. It is one of the greatest means of hearing God's voice speak to our own hearts. By it, we draw near to Him.

Martin Luther expressed it perfectly when he said, "Nothing is more perilous than to be weary of the Word of God. Thinking he knows enough, a person begins little by little to despise the Word until he has lost Christ and the gospel altogether." May God forbid that ever be the case in my life or your life, Friend. We must never stop pursuing growth. It is His purpose that we continually be transformed, moving forward from strength to strength, faith to faith, and glory to glory. Do not deprive yourself. His Word is wholesome, nourishing, strengthening, preserving, and sweet. The Word of God will bring forth spiritual joy and pleasure within your spirit!

> *The rarest treasures of life are found in his truth. That's why God's Word is prized like others prize the finest gold. Sweeter also than honey are his living words—sweet words dripping from the honeycomb! – Psalm 19:10 TPT*

> *How sweet are Your words to my taste, sweeter than honey to my mouth! – Psalm 119:103 AMP*

> *Your words were found and I ate them, and Your words became a joy to me and the delight of my heart; for I have been called by Your name, O Lord God of hosts. – Jeremiah 15:16 AMP*

Matthew 5:6 says, "You're blessed when you've worked up a good appetite for God. He's food and drink in the best meal you'll ever eat" (MSG). How's your appetite? Do you hunger and thirst for the living Word of God? Many things can affect one's appetite. In the natural, filling up on junk food can ruin our appetite for good, healthy, and nutritious foods. We also exhibit certain symptoms when we are getting sick. We may begin to feel weak, puny, easily irritated, or downright miserable. If we go to the doctor in this condition, many times the doctor will ask this question, "How's your appetite?" The first few questions a doctor will ask when you take your sick child to see him might be: "Is he eating? Has there been a change in his appetite?" Why do they ask these questions? A person's appetite determines a lot of things. If we haven't had much of an appetite for His Word, it might just be time to examine the heart. It could very well be a symptom of a lingering condition of the inner man. It could be an indication that there is healing that needs to take place within the deepest recesses of the heart. Some things within the soul may need to be restored to health. And the Word of God is always the prescription for the issues of the spiritual heart.

Today, the Lord is extending this invitation to you and to me:

> *Taste and see that the LORD is good. How happy is the person who takes refuge in him! — Psalm 34:8 CSB*

Let's taste His Word, not just once but over and over and over again. Feast with plenty. Regularly consume pure spiritual milk. Latch onto the Word of God. Receive the good seed and drink in the rain of His Spirit.

Are you hungry? Are you thirsty?

> *For He satisfies the thirsty and fills the hungry with good things. — Psalm 107:9 NLT*

PRAYER

Lord, increase my hunger and thirst for You and Your Word! Speak to my heart. I long to hear Your voice. I'll hold onto every word. Heal me and restore me. Soak me and saturate me. Fill me and continue to refill me again and again. May the Word of Your mouth become a joy to me and the delight of my heart. And may Your Word become sweeter than honey on my own lips. Thank You, Lord, that Your Word will not return to You unfulfilled. Have Your way in my heart and my life! Cause me to grow in a way that lifts me to new heights in Jesus's name. Amen!

"We can see that this 'milk' is the Lord himself dispensed to us in the Word of God. Our craving for this 'milk' is not only because of necessity but of delight. He is the Seed, the Word, the Milk, the Lord, and the Living Stone." – The Passion Translation; Footnote (b); 1 Peter 2:1-3

UnStuck—I've Found The Recipe For Being Happy

Full of Sap

*Listen! Are you thirsty for more? Come to the refreshing waters and drink.
Even if you have no money, come, buy, and eat. Yes, come and buy all the
wine and milk you desire—it won't cost a thing. Why spend your hard-
earned money on something that can't nourish you or work so hard for
something that can't satisfy? So listen carefully to me and you'll enjoy a
sumptuous feast, delighting in the finest of food. Pay attention and come
closer to me, and hear, that your total being may flourish.*

Isaiah 55:1-3a TPT

Lord, we accept Your invitation! We're listening. Our ears are
attuned to Your voice, and we are leaning in close. Jesus, You have
our full attention.

This wine in Isaiah chapter fifty-five can symbolize the joy-
filled blessings of God. And this milk can symbolize the spiritual
nourishment we receive from God's Word. The subtitle for Isaiah
chapter fifty-five, found in many translations, reads "An Invitation to
an Abundant Life." The Lord desires for us to have this abundant life.
He delights in giving good gifts to His children. It is His desire that we
not only grow but also absolutely flourish!

*Blessed is the man who walks not in the counsel of the wicked, nor
stands in the way of sinners, nor sits in the seat of scoffers; but his
delight is in the law of the Lord, and on his law he meditates day
and night. He is like a tree planted by streams of water that yields its*

fruit in its season, and its leaf does not wither. In all that he does, he prospers. — Psalm 1:1-3 ESV

I don't know about you, but I love the Word of God. I can't get enough of it! The Bible is full of promises for those who hunger, thirst, and delight in God's Word. Like the rain of Isaiah 55:10-11, we need His Word to grow and thrive. Like the milk of 1 Peter 2:1-3, we need His Word to sustain us spiritually. So, we partake of it and draw from it frequently and regularly. Meditating on the Word daily causes us to become like a tree firmly planted. No matter what winds of adversity rage around it, it remains secure and stable. Not only is the tree described in Psalms chapter one and verse three firmly planted, but it is also planted where its roots receive an abundance of water. It is a well-nourished tree that is continually refreshed. It's a thriving tree that is yielding fruit! Its leaf does not wither, but it is green and flourishing. And the man or woman who is like this tree is blessed and prospers.

The word "blessed" in this text is the word *'esher* in the original Hebrew language, and it translates as "happy." Matthew Henry says that the blessings that come to this devoted believer are "enough to make him completely happy; none of the ingredients of happiness shall be wanting to him."

Blessed

We become like a well-watered, thriving tree that continues to be fruitful and whose leaf does not dry up and wither. We prosper in all that we do. The word for "prosper" in verse three is the word *tsalach* in the original Hebrew language, and it means "to breakout, push forward, make progress, and succeed." The Lord will see to it that we prosper.

Jeremiah 17:7-8 says, "But blessed are those who trust in the Lord and have made the Lord their hope and confidence. They are like trees planted along a riverbank, with roots that reach deep into the water. Such trees are not bothered by the heat or worried by long months of drought. Their leaves stay green, and they never stop producing fruit" (NLT).

Do you have a good root system? Do your roots go deep? We must be planted in Christ and rooted in the Word of God. Keep drawing from His Word and tapping into His presence, Friend. We were meant to be full, healthy, and thriving!

In the natural sense, water is drawn up from the roots as sap. It is the evaporation of water at the leaves that is believed to be the main force that draws it up from the roots. Listen, it's in the dry times when you feel all used up that this process kicks in. If we cry out to God, return to His Word, and tell Him that we are dry and thirsty, He promises to fill us again and again. Even the smallest leaf of the believer should be full of the sap of the Holy Spirit. In the natural, the sap is the lifeblood of the plant. Water and minerals come up through the roots. The plant excretes sap from the roots to the leaves, and it does so through pressure within the plant. This pressure or tension is called cohesion. Like pressure within a plant, pressure and tension can be extremely important in our lives as well. Under these circumstances, we grow. Without any challenges, we remain the same. You can be sure that God wants to use these times in our lives for our good as well as the good of others.

What happens next in this process of plant life is that the water escapes through the leaves into the atmosphere. Clouds form, rain falls from the clouds, and you know the rest of the cycle. Right? The whole earth depends on this. What I'm saying is that we should be tapping into the Word of God and the presence of God regularly, being so full of the Spirit of God that what He has put on the inside of us overflows into the atmosphere around us, the people around us, and the world around us until it brings life to everything it touches. Jesus said in John 7:37-38, "If anyone thirsts, let him come to Me and drink. He who believes in Me, as the Scripture has said, out of his heart will flow rivers of living water."

I love what John Gill says about this living water that you and I have received. He says it is called "living" water "because by it dead sinners are quickened, drooping saints are revived, and comforted; spiritual life in them is maintained and supported, and it springs up to, and issues in eternal life: and it is expressed by 'rivers' of living water, because of the abundance of it in regeneration, justification, and pardon; it is grace for grace, abundance of grace believers receive from Christ; and from him, in whom those large measures of grace are, they 'flow out' again."

Thank You, Lord, for this living water!

What has been flowing out of your heart? Are we so full of the living water that, like a river full of abundant supply, we diffuse what we have received to others? The Bible makes it clear that as we come and drink this living water, we become a channel of blessing to others. What we have received from Christ is to flow out of our hearts through our communication with others, our testimony, our prayers, our love, and the grace and compassion we extend to others. It is to be demonstrated in our actions and even by our response in times of tension and pressure. Whatever is in the heart will flow out.

In plant life, this flow can be disrupted by bubbles or voids within the plant that is referred to as vapor cavities in a liquid-free zone. It's like what happens when air gets in a gas line or gas tank and disrupts the flow. Has there been anything in your life that has been disrupting your flow? Every area of our lives needs to be saturated with the water of the Word and the Holy Spirit—no gaps or pockets left untouched. What areas of your life do you need this water of His Spirit to touch and fill today?

> They shall be full of sap [of spiritual vitality] and [rich in the]
> verdure [of trust, love, and contentment.] – Psalm 92:14b – AMPC

 PRAYER

Lord, today, I come to you hungry and thirsty. Nourish my very soul. Refresh me and strengthen me, I pray. Fill every empty place of my heart, Lord. Saturate me until no area of my life is left untouched by You. And then let the richness that You have filled me with spill out and spill over into others' lives. Let it be a God-touch from Your living water flowing out from a life transformed by Your power and tangible presence. Let Your Spirit bring life and vitality to the dry, the thirsty, the hurting, and the empty that I encounter in my everyday life. As You impact and bless my life, use me as an instrument in Your very own hands.

Yahweh will always guide you where to go and what to do. He will fill you with refreshment even when you are in a dry, difficult place. He will continually restore strength to you, so you will flourish like a well-watered garden and like an ever-flowing, trustworthy spring of blessing. – Isaiah 58:11 TPT

Press On

For as the days of a tree are the days of my people, and mine elect shall long enjoy the work of their hands.

– Isaiah 65:22b KJV

In many scriptures, God's people are compared to trees, even flourishing and thriving plants. One of the characteristics of a tree is that it stores up sap to be used in the next season. If we can keep this picture in our spirit, we will realize that no season is ever wasted. God has something for us in every season.

In the winter season, trees are producing sap. The sap is being collected and stored. You may not be able to physically see this process, but I assure you that something significant is happening on the inside. Sweet sap will be available for the next season. Ironically, the harsher the winter season is, the better the following growing season will be.

You may be walking through a difficult season in your life right now, or maybe you have just come through a particularly trying one. Can we thrive even in these difficult seasons of our lives? The answer is yes! God wants us to be full and flourishing in every season of our lives. We will go through hard winter seasons. Then the season will shift again, but let's not miss what God has for us in the hard seasons as well as the trouble-free, enjoyable seasons. And let's not think for one minute that He is not doing a significant work on the inside.

Lessons from Nature

The difference between summer sap and winter sap within a tree is the flow of the sap. The best flow actually happens before the buds have even begun to physically appear. With rising temperatures in the spring, pressure is created within the tree that will force the sap out of any holes in the tree. Sap will even flow out of broken branches. Like a tree, you and I will continue to grow and flow right in the midst of our difficulties and brokenness. When we continue to fill ourselves with His Word and His presence, we will flourish and thrive even in the midst of our fiercest struggles.

In nature, certain elements like wind and shorter days of daylight affect the trees. Cold seasons, dark seasons, and dry seasons cause leaves to wither up and fall off, but according to Psalms chapter one and verse three, our leaves will not wither. Why? Because there is a sufficient supply of living water available to us! Sometimes we may feel like we are dry and withering, but those are just feelings. We have to get to the place where we no longer live in our feelings. Let's just go ahead and believe every Word that God has spoken!

Jeremiah 17:8 says, "For he will be [nourished] like a tree planted by the waters, that spreads out its roots by the river; and will not fear the heat when it comes; but its leaves will be green and moist. And it will not be anxious and concerned in a year of drought nor stop bearing fruit" (AMP).

Like that tree, we will not be overcome by the heat of fiery trials. We will continue to draw from the Lord's strength and His hidden support. His river does not run dry. We may *feel* the effects of trials, but we will not be damaged by them. Instead, we will grow all the more under them. The Scripture says that your leaf shall remain green! This word "green" means "fresh and flourishing." We can continue to thrive, flourish, and produce fruit in spite of it all, Friend!

It's so important that we get our hearts and minds right toward our troubles. In the book of Philippians, the apostle Paul said that he counted all his struggles as dung.

> *But what things were gain to me, those I counted loss for Christ. Yea doubtless, and I count all things but loss for the excellency of the knowledge of Christ Jesus my Lord: for whom I have suffered the loss of all things, and do count them but dung, that I may win Christ. – Philippians 3:7-8 KJV*

Thayer's Greek-English Lexicon of the New Testament translates this word "dung" as the excrement of animals. The Passion Translation actually uses the word manure.

> *Yet all of the accomplishments that I once took credit for, I've now forsaken them and I regard it all as nothing compared to the delight of experiencing Jesus Christ as my Lord! To truly know him meant letting go of everything from my past and throwing all my boasting on the garbage heap. It's all like a pile of manure to me now, so that I may be enriched in the reality of knowing Jesus Christ and embrace him as Lord in all of his greatness. – Philippians 3:7-8 TPT*

Paul took a lot of hard hits. He suffered a lot of losses, and he says that he considered all those things as dung or manure. The idea here is that Paul considered these losses as completely unworthy to even look back upon in comparison to truly knowing Christ and experiencing Him as Lord. I cannot help but wonder if Paul also considered these trials as the very fertilizer upon the soil of his heart, his walk, and his ministry.

Animal manure has been used for centuries as fertilizer for farming and is a great organic fertilizer. It enriches and improves the soil structure so that the soil holds more nutrients and water. It has numerous benefits like promoting the soil's trace mineral supply, improving plant nutrition, and aiding in plant growth. It is commonly used to replenish soil with depleted nitrogen levels. Can we just for a moment entertain the idea that trials and difficulties become the very richest of fertilizers thrown upon our lives, causing some of the greatest growth and fruit to emerge as a result?

Paul was so focused on the priceless value of knowing Christ that not only did he stop mourning his losses but even his human achievements became insignificant to him also. He wanted nothing more than "to know Christ and experience the mighty power that raised him from the dead." He went as far as saying that he desired to suffer with Him, sharing in His death.

> *And this, so that I may know Him [experientially, becoming more thoroughly acquainted with Him, understanding the remarkable wonders of His Person more completely] and [in that same way experience] the power of His resurrection [which overflows and is active in believers], and [that I may share] the fellowship of His sufferings, by being continually conformed [inwardly into His likeness even] to His death [dying as He did!]; so that I may attain to the resurrection [that will raise me] from the dead. – Philippians 3:10b-11 AMP*

Paul said that he pressed on so that he might reach the purpose for which Christ Jesus laid hold of him to make him His own (verse 12). For Paul, that meant letting go of everything in his past that would no longer serve him well in his future.

> *But one thing I do: forgetting what lies behind and reaching forward to what lies ahead, I press on toward the goal to win the (heavenly) prize of the upward call of God in Jesus. – Philippians 3:13b-14 AMP*

Is there anything that you need to let go of from your past? Today is a good day to let go of it and leave it behind. Press on! And when things feel dry or difficult, keep on keeping on. Keep doing what you know to do even when it's hard. Trust God and trust His process.

He will fill you with refreshment even when you are in a dry, difficult place. He will continually restore strength to you. – Isaiah 58:11 TPT

 **PRAYER**

Lord, I thank You that even in the place of pressure and brokenness in my life, the sweet sap of Your Spirit can flow from my heart because I have stored up Your Word. Because my relationship with you is real and my roots go deep, my life remains full even in the midst of difficulties. Troubles become the very fertilizer upon the soil of my heart. You make all things abound in me. It's Your power that conforms me to Your likeness, refreshes me when I'm dry and weary, and restores my strength and vitality. You continually sustain me. You bring all things in my life to a good success. Today, I let go of my past and press forward with great hope. Oh, that I might know You more intimately and understand more clearly Your remarkable wonders! Nothing compares to the delight of experiencing You as my Lord.

So let's not get tired of doing good. At just the right time we will reap a harvest of blessing if we don't give up. – Galatians 6:9 NLT

Stronger with Every Step Forward

How enriched are they who find their strength in the Lord; within their hearts are the highways of holiness! Even when their paths wind through the dark valley of tears, they dig deep to find a pleasant pool where others find only pain. He gives to them a brook of blessing filled from the rain of an outpouring. They grow stronger and stronger with every step forward, and the God of all gods will appear before them in Zion.

– Psalm 84:5-7 TPT

Sometimes we find ourselves in dry and difficult places. This is when we need to dig deep and tap into His living waters. God will refresh us and lead us forward. With every step forward, we will grow stronger and stronger! But forward movement isn't always easy, especially when we are weighed down with many grievances and burdens. So, what do we do when we feel stuck: stuck in our pain, stuck in our disappointment, stuck in our frustration, stuck in our fears or doubts, or stuck in our sin?

Like Paul, sometimes we have to leave some things behind us and simply press forward. Paul said that pressing forward for him meant letting go of the past. We must become good releasers; otherwise, we will become weighed down. Those weights make forward movement even more difficult. Is there anything in your heart that has been weighing you down? Is there anything at all that has been keeping you from moving forward?

> *Therefore we also, since we are surrounded by so great a cloud of witnesses, let us lay aside every weight, and the sin which so easily ensnares us, and let us run with endurance the race that is set before us, looking unto Jesus, the author and finisher of our faith, who for the joy that was set before Him endured the cross, despising the shame, and has sat down at the right hand of the throne of God. – Hebrews 12:1-2 NKJV*

Hebrews chapter twelve tells us to lay aside every weight and the sin that so easily ensnares us. These words "lay aside every weight" can be translated as "get rid of every arrow tip in us." The implication is of carrying an arrow on the inside, a wound that weighs us down and keeps us from running our race with freedom. The Passion Translation puts it this way: "So we must let go of every wound that has pierced us and the sin we so easily fall into" (Hebrews 12:1 TPT).

Wounds

There are many things that can cause us to become burdened, but emotional pain is something that we tend to carry. Anything that has been weighing us down puts us at a disadvantage and impedes our progress. We simply cannot continue to replay the emotional pain. We cannot continue to rehash or rehearse our offense. And we must stop blaming *whomever* for being the reason why we are where we are right now. We must stop counting our losses and press forward with endurance. According to verse two, we do it like this:

> *We look away from the natural realm and we fasten our gaze onto Jesus who birthed faith within us and who leads us forward into faith's perfection. – Hebrews 12:2 TPT*

Have you been hurt? Have you caught some bad breaks? Have you been used and abused? The Bible tells us that in the midst of these occasions, we must consider our Lord, Jesus, lest we become worn down and cave under life's pressures.

> *For consider Him who endured such hostility from sinners against Himself, lest you become weary and discouraged in your souls. – Hebrews 12:3 NKJV*

The Message Bible says it like this: "Keep your eyes on Jesus, who both began and finished this race we're in. Study how he did it. Because he never lost sight of where he was headed—that exhilarating finish in and with God—he could put up with anything along the way: cross, shame, whatever. And now he's there, in the place of honor, right alongside God. When you find yourselves flagging in your faith, go over that story again, item by item, that long litany of hostility he plowed through. That will shoot adrenaline into your souls!"

Verses four through eleven go on to say, "In this all-out match against sin, others have suffered far worse than you, to say nothing of what Jesus went through—all that bloodshed! So don't feel sorry for yourselves."

Don't feel sorry for yourself! Self-pity is your own worst enemy. It will keep you in a stuck place far too long.

> *[Reckon up and consider it all in comparison with your trials], so that you may not grow weary or exhausted, losing heart and relaxing and fainting in your minds. You have not yet struggled and fought agonizingly against sin, nor have you yet resisted and withstood to the point of pouring out your [own] blood. – Hebrews 12:3-4 AMPC*

Don't lose your perspective during a time of personal struggle! God will take the most difficult and painful events of your life and use them to educate you and prepare you. And He will even do it when the painful events happen to be the consequences of your own doing. God will at times correct you then heal you and set you free so you can rise to a new level in your personal growth. Hebrews 12:5-11 describes God's correction and discipline as a demonstration of His love toward His children.

> *My dear child, don't shrug off God's discipline, but don't be crushed by it either. It's the child he loves that he disciplines; the child he embraces, he also corrects. God is educating you; that's why you must never drop out. He's treating you as dear children. This trouble you're in isn't punishment: it's training, the normal experience of children. – Hebrews 12:5-7 MSG*

God is training us. Sometimes that training may be in the form of correction and discipline, and that can be painful. Nevertheless, we should fully embrace it so we can truly live.

> *God is doing what is best for us, training us to live God's holy best. – Hebrews 12:10b MSG*

God's Word encourages us that although training and correction may seem painful at the time, "afterward it yields the peaceable fruit of righteousness to those who have been trained by it" (Hebrews 12:11 KJV). For the believer yielded to the Lord, trouble isn't punishment. What you endure is meant to educate you. It's training, instruction, and preparation that leads to maturity, life, vitality, freedom, and happiness, and it yields a good harvest!

The word "yields" in Hebrews chapter twelve and verse eleven translates as "gives again, performs, restores, and rewards." This training that comes out of our troubles pays off! It gives the advantage back to us. Today, let's dig deep. And let's move forward into times of refreshing.

> *Let your eyes look directly forward, and your gaze be straight before you. – Proverbs 4:25 ESV*

 **PRAYER**

Lord, I am letting go of the past, and I'm pressing forward. Lift the burdens of my heart as I cast aside the heavy weights. Heal my wounds as I surrender them to You. Thank You, Lord, for You strengthen me and enrich my life. Refresh me once again, Lord, with the rain of Your Spirit. I will embrace Your plan for my life, for I know that it is good. Thank You, Lord, for enduring the cross of Calvary. Today, I consider Your great sacrifice, the pain and grief You endured, and the blood that You shed for me. I am humbled. And I am grateful. Thank You, Lord, for teaching me and instructing me in the ways of life, freedom, and happiness. And thank you for the promised harvest in Jesus's name.

Do not yield to fear, for I am always near. Never turn your gaze from me, for I am your faithful God. I will infuse you with my strength and help you in every situation. I will hold you firmly with my victorious right hand. – Isaiah 41:10 TPT

Courageous Self-Recovery in God's Strength

So be made strong even in your weakness by lifting up your tired hands in prayer and worship. And strengthen your weak knees, for as you keep walking forward on God's paths all your stumbling ways will be divinely healed!

– Hebrews 12:12-13 TPT

Hebrews chapter twelve is such a powerful chapter of instruction, encouragement, hope, and promise for the believer who has become weary. I refer to it as being battle weary. In other words, the believer has experienced one battle after another. The season of battles has become long, and he is worn out from bearing up under such difficulties, trials, conflicts, and afflictions. Alongside Hebrews chapter twelve in my Bible is a note that reads, "The duty to which the writer urges his readers is courageous self-recovery in God's strength." It does take courage to acknowledge the condition of our own hearts and confront our own issues. It does take courage to forget the past, let go of hurt and offense, cast aside sin, and keep moving forward with endurance. Life happens, and we are continually faced with things we must process, things that can put a believer's heart in a place of great discouragement and even despair. In Hebrews chapter twelve, verses twelve and thirteen speak to this very situation.

So then, brace up and reinvigorate and set right your slackened and weakened and drooping hands and strengthen your feeble and palsied and tottering knees, and cut through and make firm and plain and smooth, straight paths for your feet [yes, make them safe and upright and happy paths that go in the right direction], so that the lame and halting [limbs] may not be put out of joint, but rather may be cured. – Hebrews 12:13-14 AMPC

This is a clear picture of weariness and being utterly exhausted from trials. Slackened, weakened, and drooping hands are those of the Christian who is completely discouraged. Their heart is sinking under the weight of burdens. They are feeling absolutely defeated. The feeble, weak, or trembling knees represent the Christian who feels as if they cannot keep going. Their strength is gone. And the trial seems to have left them with a limp. Those who have lost hope are compared to those who have palsy-stricken limbs. The word "feeble" here literally means "paralyzed." Have you experienced something so difficult that it has left you emotionally and spiritually paralyzed for a time? I have. It took a lot of perseverance on my part to recover and regain even more strength than I previously knew and walked in before. When we feel like we've been knocked down and plowed over, we cannot stay down for the count. The apostle Paul exhorts us in these passages to take courage during times when our own heart seems to be fainting. We must get up, shake ourselves, and press forward.

Regarding this passage in Hebrews, *The Pulpit Commentary* states that the "hands" and "knees" and "feet" represent the powers of "action, motion, and progression." Clearly, the description of the hands, knees, and feet in these verses reflects the inward condition of the heart. And here we are urged to brace up and reinvigorate our hearts. Most translations use the words "lift up" and "strengthen." The word "strengthen" in this text literally means "to restore to a right state, to lift up that which is out of its proper place and posture, to renew the life of, and to revive." It is the word *anorthoo* in the original Greek language, and it comes from the same word from which we derive our English word *orthopedic*. In these scriptures, we are urged to make straight paths for our feet so that what has become lame (injured and halted) will not be put out of joint, injured even more, or made worse! You see, we cannot afford to remain in this downcast condition, Friend. Most translations, including the King James version, use the term "turned out of the way" or "put out of joint." The Greek word *ektrepo* is used for this term and it means to turn, twist, or be dislocated. Medical writers used this word when referring to the setting of dislocated parts of the body. It is a picture of one setting a dislocated limb or broken bone. And this word that is used here appears in the imperative tense, calling for the resetting and restoration to be done now. Do it right away. Do not delay! The time is now.

We are talking about becoming lame in a spiritual sense. Paul is charging us to no longer allow the trials and adversity in our lives to spiritually paralyze us or cause us to get stuck. Have the events that have taken place in your life caused you to be thrown out of joint or moved from your former steadfast posture? Gather up your courage and exercise some self-recovery in God's strength! Find your feet again. Make level paths so that you will not be tripped up and stumble the next time you face a battle. Be healed. Be encouraged! Receive fresh strength!

> "The hands fall, and the knees tremble, and the heart sinks within us. But confidence in God and the hope of heaven and the assurance that all this is for our good will reinvigorate the enfeebled frame, and enable us to bear what we once supposed would crush us to the dust. A courageous mind braces a feeble body, and hope makes it fresh for new conflicts." – Albert Barnes

A Courageous Mind

Ray Stedman makes this statement about Hebrews chapter twelve: "The writer is calling for his readers to 'deal first with yourselves. Get your hearts right toward your troubles.'" Dealing with our own hearts and keeping our hearts right toward our troubles are two vital ingredients for spiritual health and happiness. The following verses provide more instructions for experiencing lives that grow, flourish, and thrive.

Pursue peace with all people, and holiness, without which no one will see the Lord: looking carefully lest anyone fall short of the grace of God; lest any root of bitterness springing up cause trouble, and by this many become defiled. – Hebrews 12:14-15 NKJV

Keep a sharp eye out for weeds of bitter discontent. A thistle or two gone to seed can ruin a whole garden in no time. – Hebrews 12:15 MSG

We have been asking our gardener, God, to landscape our hearts with His Word, making a beautiful salvation garden of our lives. Hebrews 12:14 reveals two things that can ruin a garden: roots of bitterness and weeds of discontent. This is why it is so important for us to leave the past in the past, forgive and let go, and press forward even when it's difficult. This is also why we must learn to quickly submit to God's discipline and correction and be restored to spiritual health. We do it so that "what is lame may not be dislocated, but rather be healed."

Healed— made whole, cured, set at one again, freed from sin and error

Verses twenty-five through twenty-nine of Hebrews chapter twelve speaks of the shaking of anything that *can* be shaken. This refers in part to the removal of things that can be shaken so only the things that are essential to our spiritual health, strength, and eternity will remain. The Message Bible refers to this shaking as "actively cleaning house." This shaking loose of anything that is detrimental to our Christian walk frees us up to receive all that God has for us. All this realignment and healing of the heart is a huge part of getting fresh strength! Do you need fresh strength today?

For God is not an indifferent bystander. He's actively cleaning house, torching all that needs to burn, and he won't quit until it's all cleansed. God himself is Fire! – Hebrews 12:29 MSG

 **PRAYER**

Shake everything loose that's not of You, Lord! I fully submit my heart to You. I will lift up my hands unto the Lord in the heat of the battle. I will bow my knees in prayer. I will keep walking forward on the path that You have chosen and set before me. I take courage and deal with roots of bitterness and weeds of discontentment. I lay an axe to them now in Jesus's name. I choose to forgive, let go, leave the past in the past, and press forward. I put my hands to the plow, and I won't look back. Meet me right where I'm at today, Lord. Bring about this realignment and healing in my heart and spirit. Restore my spiritual health. And give me fresh strength.

Dear friend, listen well to my words; tune your ears to my voice. Keep my message in plain view at all times. Concentrate! Learn it by heart. Those who discover these words live, really live; body and soul, they're bursting with health. – Proverbs 4:20-22 MSG

Fresh and Flourishing

The righteous shall flourish like a palm tree, he shall grow like a cedar in Lebanon. Those who are planted in the house of the Lord, shall flourish in the courts of our God. They shall still bear fruit in old age; they shall be fresh and flourishing.

– Psalm 92:12-14 NKJV

Flourish—Break forth as a bud, bloom, spread, grow, sprout, break out, increase, enlarge

We were meant to flourish! Psalm 92:12 says that a person in right standing with God will flourish like a palm tree and grow like a cedar in Lebanon. Friend, you need to know that flourishing palm trees grow upright under the greatest pressures and with enormous weight upon them. The fronds at the tops of these trees alone can weigh hundreds of pounds each, yet they seem to grow all the more under the weight. They don't bend or bow but they grow straight up toward heaven. The tree has such elasticity that it grows upward even while loaded down with the tremendous amount of weight it bears. It has the kind of elasticity that allows it to bend over almost level to the ground during violent storms. Then it returns to its original posture and position. A palm tree's genetic makeup allows it to be incredibly flexible. At the top of the palms are branches or leaves called fronds. These fronds are turned upwards and resemble raised arms in worship. A palm tree has a root system that spreads out far and wide, making it completely stable. In Scripture, the palm is always referencing the date palm.

The date palm has deep tap roots called a root ball. This root system gives the tree the ability to flourish even in dry and difficult climates. What I find truly amazing is that these palms are simply unaffected by the harsh seasons and harsh elements that will destroy other kinds of trees. You would think that these palm trees would be ripped from the ground during hurricanes, but they are not! Cyclones will not even uproot most of them. They are sturdy. They are resilient. And palm trees are often described as being graceful. They have a gracefulness about them. It is gracefulness wedded to strength. That's what it is!

As moisture is being drawn up through the roots of most trees, the sap moves through the outside layer between the bark and the wood. Within a palm, however, the sap moves through the very center of the tree. Because it moves through the very heart of the palm, the tree will survive if the bark is damaged. It will survive even if inches of the bark are completely removed around the tree. Other trees will die under these circumstances, but the palm tree is simply not affected by any surface damage. These palm trees are thriving under all conditions. A palm is also a fruit-bearing tree. Not only is its fruit remarkably nutritious, but the older the palm tree gets the sweeter its fruit!

> *The righteous shall flourish like a palm tree, he shall grow like a cedar in Lebanon. – Psalm 92:12a NKJV*

How does a cedar in Lebanon grow? It grows taller and higher than other trees. Growing to a height of one hundred feet, the cedars of Lebanon are the tallest trees in the region. They grow steadily. They can even grow in the snow. The cedar of Lebanon has incorruptible wood. In First Kings chapter six and verse eighteen, we can read about the temple of God's presence being built entirely out of cedarwood. The wood was transported over two hundred miles. A lot of effort went into acquiring the wood and transporting it. Cedarwood was known for its durability and even its resistance to rotting. William Lithgow's *The Totall Discourse of the Rare Adventures and Painefull Peregrinations of Long Nineteene Years Travayles* has some fascinating notes in it about the roots of some of these cedar trees in Lebanon. Lithgow says that these trees are so grounded and so rooted that it's almost impossible to destroy them. In fact, shepherds in Lebanon have made fires and even holes in many of the trees where they sleep, and yet these same trees will continue to flourish. Think about that! And they will still bear cones when they have been split apart by lightning or torn by the wind. Like palm trees, cedars can withstand violent storms. As far as fruit-bearing goes, the cedars of Lebanon will continue to bear fruit for centuries even after other types of trees have decayed. The cedars are always green and very fragrant. Their fruit is said to be wholesome fruit, tasting like apples but sweeter. Every part of the tree is useful. A cedar in Lebanon will have a long and useful life. And God's Word says that you and I are like a palm tree and like a cedar in Lebanon.

Much like what Scripture is presenting here, the trees are continuously green and continue to produce fruit even in old age. Other trees stop bearing fruit when they are old, but it is the aged palm trees that bear the heaviest clusters of fruit. In Lebanon's cedar forests, trees over the age of 1,000 years old are still thriving.

> *The righteous shall flourish like a palm tree, He shall grow like a cedar in Lebanon. Those who are planted in the house of the Lord Shall flourish in the courts of our God. They shall still bear fruit in old age; They shall be fresh and flourishing. – Psalm 92:12-14 NKJV*

Matthew Henry says, "The last days of the saints are sometimes their best days, and their last work is their best work." I believe that! We are, indeed, flourishing much like palm trees and growing in so many ways like the cedars in Lebanon. Dr. Thomason's book entitled *Land and the Book* describes some remarkable things about cedars in Lebanon. He says that young trees are constantly springing up from the roots of old ones and from seeds of ripe cones. He has seen these infant cedars in the thousands just springing up from the soil. You and I are like the resilient, durable, fruitful cedar. Let's lay down a good foundation and a rich spiritual heritage for our children and our grandchildren. The endurance that we exercise as we are faithful in our walk with God today will produce a harvest that continues beyond our years. Don't you dare quit, saint of God. Generations to come are counting on you.

> *May the Lord cause you to flourish, both you and your children.*
> *– Psalms 115:14 NIV*

You shall flourish like a palm tree and grow like a cedar in Lebanon. You shall increase and be full, healthy, vibrant, and enlarged. Palms are said to be self-cleaning because they shed their dead leaves and seem to know just the right time to do it. And the cedars in Lebanon know how to recover and heal. Their sap acts as a healing agent. If the tree's trunk gets a gash in it, the sap will cover the gash and harden, providing a barrier for protection, aiding in its healing. It will even protect it from fungi and harmful insects. The wood has a strong fragrance that will repel most insects, and any insects that try to eat its leaves will be killed by its sap. That sap heals and protects! And so does the sap of His Spirit.

Are you struggling in this season with the many storms of life? Storms will come. Hold on! No matter what you are facing now or what you may face in the future, dig in deep and stay full of the sap of His spirit! You were meant to thrive even in the thick of it. Continue to abide in God's presence and draw from Him. Become more devoted to the Lord than you are devoted to anyone or anything else, and you will grow in victory and stand in strength!

> *Yes! Look how you've made all your devoted lovers to flourish like*
> *palm trees, each one growing in victory, standing with strength!*
> *You've transplanted them into your heavenly courtyard, where they*
> *are thriving before you, for in your presence they will still overflow*
> *and be anointed. Even in their old age they will stay fresh, bearing*
> *luscious fruit and abiding faithfully. – Psalm 92:12-14 TPT*

PRAYER

Lord, thank You for giving me the ability to not only survive but also thrive. You continually sustain me. I experience steady growth in my life because of Your generous supply. You cause me to grow, bloom, flourish, and thrive even under what feels like the weight of the world sometimes. Help me, Lord, to bounce back quickly like a palm tree after the storm. Cause me to recover and heal when life cuts like a knife. Help me to know when to shed the dead things in my life. Cause me to become more resilient and bear good fruit. And may my life be a Christ-like fragrance rising up to God.

The trees of the Lord are watered abundantly and are filled with sap, the cedars of Lebanon which He has planted. – Psalm 104:16 AMPC

Store Up the Word of God

Your word I have treasured and stored in my heart,
that I may not sin against You.

– Psalm 119:11 AMP

In His Word, God likens us to a garden, a tree, flourishing plants whose leaves shall be green and shall not cease from yielding fruit even in old age. We have been focusing on allowing God, our gardener, to landscape our lives with His Word, making us a beautiful, vibrant, and fragrant salvation garden. It's one that's flourishing, always green, always producing, and whose leaves are full of sap. The key to thriving is being rooted and grounded in the Word of God and meditating on it day and night. We receive a continual flow of His fresh strength. The Word can bring such a refreshing to our dry and weary souls. Our spiritual vitality is renewed. His Word is the main ingredient for every recipe! It's food for the soul. By it, we are well-nourished, strengthened, and sustained. It quickens our spirits and revives our hearts. We are enriched and blessed when we follow His precepts. By His Word, we grow, flourish, and even thrive. His words are sweeter than honey, bringing joy and delight to the heart. His Word provides hope, encouragement, support, and stability. Through the Word of God, we find correction and direction. We come into alignment with His plans, purposes, and blessings. The Word of God is a cleansing agent, cleansing and purifying us day after day.

For he died for us, sacrificing himself, to make us holy and pure,
cleansing us through the showering of the pure water of the Word of
God. – Ephesians 5:25b-26 TPT

The Word of God convicts the heart and brings about real transformation
in the life of the believer. And His Word keeps us from sinning.

Your word I have hidden in my heart, that I might not sin against
You. – Psalm 119:11 NKJV

The word "hidden" in this Scripture translates as "to store up as a
treasure." The Passion Translation puts it like this: "I consider your
Word to be my greatest treasure, and I treasure it in my heart to keep
me from committing sin's treason against you." Do we consider the Word
of God to be our greatest treasure? Are we storing it up in our hearts?

> "David treasured the Word of God in his heart as the most
> valuable thing to him. He not only heard the word and read the
> word but he received it into his affections; mixed it with faith,
> laid it up in his mind and memory for future use; preserved it
> in his heart as a choice treasure, where it might dwell richly,
> and be of service to him on many occasions; and particularly be
> of use against temptation to sin." – *John Gill's Exposition of the*
> *Entire Bible*

Ephesians 6:17 refers to the Word of God as the sword of the Spirit,
a mighty weapon to be used against the assaults of the enemy. It is
essentially one of the most important pieces of the armor of God. It is
a mighty tool for tearing down strongholds, and it protects us from the
temptation to sin. The Word of God dispels the lies of the enemy. It
opens our eyes to the truth, and His truth sets us free. Hebrews chapter
four and verse twelve refers to the Word of God as a two-edged sword.

For the Word of God is living and active, sharper than any two-
edged sword, piercing to the division of soul and spirit, of joints

and marrow, and discerning the thoughts and intentions of the heart. – Hebrews 4:12 ESV

This spiritual two-edged sword penetrates the deepest parts of our nature. It discerns even the thoughts and intentions of our hearts. It allows us to see the parts of ourselves that are not pleasing to the Lord. It reveals the things in our hearts that have been hindering and halting our progress and blocking the blessings. It is a two-edged sword. His Word judges as well as heals the heart of the believer. This sword reaches the very core of our inner-being, causing us to deal with error and sin in our lives. John Darby says that the Word of God is "an instrument which, in its operations, does not allow the desires of the flesh and of the mind liberty to act; which does not permit the heart to deceive itself; but which procures us strength, and places us without any consciousness of evil in the presence of God, to pursue our course with joy and spiritual energy."

Ephesians chapter six describes the Word of God as a sword in the hands of the believer faced with spiritual warfare. It leaves us with a picture of a Christian using it as a weapon to fight spiritual battles and gain victory. In Hebrews chapter four, we see a different aspect of this sword. The word used for "sword" can be translated as "the knife (scalpel) used by a surgeon." This leaves us with the picture of the believer becoming soul-sick and even lame in the midst of his Christian journey. The Great Physician uses His scalpel to probe and diagnose the heart's condition. Then He brings about glorious healing in the believer's heart, moving the believer to a place of wholeness, strength, and blessing.

God means what he says. What he says goes. His powerful Word is sharp as a surgeon's scalpel, cutting through everything, whether doubt or defense, laying us open to listen and obey. Nothing and no one can resist God's Word. We can't get away from it—no matter what. – Hebrews 4:12 MSG

I certainly cannot resist God's Word! I must allow it to accomplish what the Master has in mind! His Word is alive and active. It's effective and it's powerful.

> "It convinces powerfully, converts powerfully, and comforts powerfully. It is so powerful as it pulls down strongholds, to raise the dead, to make the deaf hear, the blind to see, the dumb to speak, and the lame to walk. It is powerful to batter down Satan's kingdom, and to set up the kingdom of Christ upon the ruins thereof." – Matthew Henry

Is there any reason that you would not store up the Word of God in your heart? Treasure up His Word, Friend! And then draw from your personal reservoir over and over and over again.

> *It is written, "Man shall not live by bread alone, but by every word that proceeds from the mouth of God." – Matthew 4:4 NKJV*

 **PRAYER**

Thank You, Lord, for Your Word! Your Word is my treasure. I value Your Word above anything else and I store it up in my heart. There, it dwells richly and goes to work. I honor and revere Your Word for it is the living, holy Word of God. Your Word is a lamp unto my feet and a light unto my path. It also shines light upon the areas of my heart that You desire to change and even heal. By Your Word, I am made free. Praise the name of the Lord! Your Word is a mighty weapon by which I gain victory. It is alive and active. I give You permission today, Lord, to accomplish anything that You desire in my heart and in my life through Your Word, for it is effective and powerful. Now I ask You, Father, to give me greater insight, understanding, and revelation of Your Word in Jesus's name.

> *You're only truly happy when you walk in total integrity, walking in the light of God's Word. – Psalm 119:1 TPT*

His Word Out of Your Mouth

For the mouth speaks what the heart is full of. A good man brings good things out of the good stored up in him, and an evil man brings evil things out of the evil stored up in him.

– Matthew 12:34-35 NIV

What have you been storing up in your heart? Whatever is in the heart comes out of our mouths, and for the Christian full of the Word of God, it was meant to! Psalm 1:1-3 describes the person who has literally stored up the Word of God. They meditate on it day and night. They are so full and overflowing that they have become like a tree planted by the rivers of water—flourishing and prospering in whatever they do. The word "meditate" not only means to habitually study His Word and ponder its meaning, but it also means to mutter and to speak. The *Brown-Drivers-Briggs Hebrew and English Lexicon* states that this word meditate means "to muse, to utter, to speak, and to roar." The Word of God stored in your heart is meant to come out of your mouth!

> *For what has been stored up in your hearts will be heard in the overflow of your words. – Matthew 12:34 TPT*

In the Hebrew language, Matthew 12:34 can read, "Truly the heart awakens and the mouth speaks." Has your heart been awakened? What have you been speaking out of your mouth?

In this passage of Matthew chapter twelve, Jesus was addressing the Pharisees with a strong truth regarding the consequences of one's words:

> *"But I say to you that for every idle word men may speak, they will give account of it in the day of judgment. For by your words you will be justified, and by your words you will be condemned." – Matthew 12:36-37 NKJV*

Just what exactly does the term "idle word" mean? It literally means a vain, thoughtless, useless word; it is a word that accomplishes no good. In the context of this passage, the pharisees' hearts were not right, and what they were speaking out of their mouths reflected it. The words they had spoken were false and malicious words. And Jesus told them that they would have to give an account of those words on the day of judgment. A closer look at this term helps us apply the Scripture to our own lives. In Aramaic, the term "every idle word" translates as "every untrue word." In the original Greek language, it means lazy, useless, and barren. It can also translate as "inactive" and "unemployed." We do not want to be careless with our words. Our words are powerful. The words we speak make an impact one way or another in our own lives as well as the lives of those to whom we speak. Truly, death and life are in the power of the tongue.

> *Death and life are in the power of the tongue; and they that love it shall eat the fruit thereof. – Proverbs 18:21 KJV*

The Produce of Our Words

The word used for "power" here in the original Hebrew language is the word *yad* and it translates as "a hand." Literally, it reads, "Death and life are in the hand of the tongue," implying that the words we speak deal forth life or death. Not only is it vital that we guard our minds and our hearts, but we must also learn to guard our words. Watch your mouth! Let's pay attention to what God is saying and become very conscious of what we, ourselves, are saying. His Word is always producing something. And what we speak out of our own mouths will produce something as well.

> It is the same with my word. I send it out, and it always produces fruit. It will accomplish all I want it to, and it will prosper everywhere I send it. – Isaiah 55:11 NLT

> For what has been stored up in your hearts will be heard in the overflow of your words! When virtue is stored within, the hearts of good, upright people will produce good fruit. – Matthew 12:34-35 TPT

What have your words been producing? Have you been satisfied with the consequences of your words? Isaiah 55:11 tells us that God's Word goes to work and does not return to Him void!

> So will the words that come out of my mouth not come back empty-handed. They'll do the work I sent them to do, they'll complete the assignment I gave them. – Isaiah 55:11 MSG

Two-mouthed

According to Hebrews chapter four and verse twelve, the Word of God is sharper than a two-edged sword. We've already looked at how the word sword itself translates as "scalpel" but the word "two-edged" is equally as intriguing. The term "two-edged" comes from the Greek word *distomos*. This word is a compound of the word *di*, meaning two, and *stomos*, referring to one's mouth. The phrase "two-edged sword" is describing something that is two-edged or "two-mouthed." This spiritual sword is the Word of God. And here within these verses of Scripture we see yet another aspect of how powerful His Word truly is when it is spoken by the believer.

The Word of God was first spoken out of God's mouth. When we hear His Word, we receive it into our hearts. We meditate upon it, and it is quickened within our spirits. God's creative Word releases its power within us as we receive the revelation of His truth! Our hearts are awakened. We are so stirred by His Word we can hardly contain it. We must release His Word out of our mouths because when we do, it then becomes a two-edged or two-mouthed sword. It becomes sharper! Essentially, the Word of God is a one-edged sword until it comes out of the mouth of the believer. When we give voice to the Word of God, the second edge is applied. That's double power, Friend! Power is activated and released when we come into agreement with the Word of God and speak it out of our mouths. I believe that there is something very powerful about even reading His Word out loud. One thing is for sure: Faith is stirred by hearing the Word of God spoken.

So then faith cometh by hearing, and hearing by the Word of God.
– Romans 10:17 KJV

You may hear God's Word through the preaching and teaching of church leaders (and this does ignite your faith), but there is just something about hearing your own voice speak the Word of God. Read His Word. Get it in your spirit. Believe it and stand on it! Speak it. Confess it. Pray it. Declare it. Release it! We cannot afford to be idle or inactive when it comes to the releasing of the Word of God out of our mouths. And we certainly cannot afford to repeat the lies of the enemy that we hear spoken around us by others or whispered in our ears by the enemy himself. Let's come into agreement with God and speak what He is speaking. The Word of God is meant to be two-mouthed—His mouth and our mouth working together. Don't be timid about it! S.R. Aldridge once said, "Timidity, which seals the lips, is a sower retaining the seed in his bag and allowing the waiting soil to go unblessed with golden crops." Now is not the time for timidity. Now is the time to release His Word out of your mouth.

I tell you all this secretly, but I want you to tell it publicly.
Whatever I tell you privately, you should shout for everyone to
hear. – Matthew 10:27 ERV

 PRAYER

Your Word is in my heart and on my lips! I take responsibility for the words that come out of my mouth. I will be careful with my speech. I will not speak what the enemy is speaking. I reject his lies and do not repeat them. My words come into agreement and alignment with what You are speaking, Lord, for Your words are true. Your words are right. Your words are powerful. Therefore, I will not be timid. My heart has been quickened and roused. I release Your Word out of my mouth. Like a seed, it is planted, and it begins to change the nature of things. Therefore, I will confess. I will pronounce. I will proclaim, and I will declare Your Word. Never stop speaking to me in the secret place, Lord. May the Word stored up within my heart overflow, go forth, and produce good fruit.

I'll transfer to my lips all the counsel that comes from your mouth;
I delight far more in what you tell me about living than in gathering
a pile of riches. I ponder every morsel of wisdom from you, I
attentively watch how you've done it. I relish everything you've told
me of life, I won't forget a word of it. – Psalm 119:11-13 MSG

An Energizing Force

And the word continues to be an energizing force in you who believe.
— 1 Thessalonians 2:13b TPT

We are walking, talking, faith-filled believers, and His Word continues to be an energizing force in our lives! There is power in the Word of God, and His Word produces faith. Faith is like a seed. Once it is planted, it immediately begins to take on a new nature. The seed breaks open. Sprouts begin to form. A stem begins to form, and the plant pushes upward. There is so much potential and power in the seed that not even a mound of dirt can stop it. This is why you see plants pushing through concrete, cracking sidewalks, driveways, and even paved roads!

> "When you plant a seed, God changes the nature of that seed so that it becomes a plant; and the power of life surges in that tender young plant to such a great extent that even a mountain of Earth cannot stop it from pushing upward!" – Oral Roberts

In Matthew chapter thirteen and verse thirty-two, Jesus referred to faith as a seed. He compared our faith to that of a mustard seed. Jesus said that the mustard seed is one of the smallest seeds but that when it is planted, it grows into the largest of trees. We can hear the Word of God, study the Word, know the Word, and even confess it out of our mouths, and our faith will grow. In addition, real-life opportunities are needed for our faith to increase. It's where the rubber meets the road. The disciples were up-close-and-personal eyewitnesses of Jesus's teachings, miracles, power, and authority in action. And yet they had moments when their faith was tested.

In Matthew chapter four, we find the disciples with Jesus as He is healing the multitudes of all kinds of sickness and disease. Even the demon possessed, epileptics, and paralytics were delivered and cured. In chapter eight, the disciples see Jesus heal the centurion's servant and Peter's mother-in-law. They watched Him cast out demons and set the demon possessed free with a word. As the multitudes pressed in, they witnessed Jesus heal all who were sick. Their faith must have been soaring! Immediately following these miracles, Jesus gave a command to depart to the other side. He and His disciples got in a boat and launched out across the Sea of Galilee. Jesus was exhausted and fell asleep. Then, suddenly, a violent storm arose. Waves were crashing right into the boat. The disciples—who had just witnessed Jesus demonstrate His mighty power and authority over sickness, disease, and spiritual forces of darkness—were now gripped with fear. And it was fear-filled words that came out of their mouths:

"Save us, Lord! We're going to die!" – Matthew 8:25 TPT

Their faith had just been tested by the storm. Jesus replied to their desperate cry, "Why are you so fearful, O you of little faith?" Then He arose and rebuked the winds and the sea, and at once, they became completely calm. The disciples were astounded. They were astonished. They marveled, and they questioned, "Who can this be, that even the winds and the sea obey Him?"

This inner circle of men discovered Jesus in a brand-new way that day. An opportunity for growth arose just as suddenly as the waves themselves arose. It was time for a personal application of all they had seen and heard. Jesus's words, "O you of little faith," must have pierced their hearts. Their faith was real, but Jesus knew it needed to be developed and strengthened. It was time for the disciples to really trust the Lord with their lives. Matthew Henry says, "Christ could have prevented this storm, and have ordered them a pleasant passage, but that would not have been so much for his glory and the confirmation of their faith as their deliverance was: this storm was for their sakes." Henry also suggests that Jesus "slept at this time, to try the faith of his disciples, whether they could trust him when he seemed to slight them. He slept not so much with a desire to be refreshed, as with a design to be awaked."

The disciples had seen Jesus perform miracles in others' lives, but now they needed Jesus to perform a miracle in their own lives. You see, there is a difference between knowing that Jesus *can* heal and knowing Jesus as *your* healer. There is a difference between knowing that Jesus *can* deliver and knowing Him as *your* deliverer. It is one thing to know that He *can* save and rescue. It is quite another when the one He rescues is you. The disciples had seen Jesus exercise His authority, but this time, Jesus exercised His authority on their behalf. This one test changed their relationship with Jesus. This one test deepened their trust and increased their faith. Sometimes it takes a storm to know Him in even greater ways. The disciples would surely need this new level of faith for their journey ahead. And Jesus knew.

In Luke chapter seventeen, the disciples became aware of the weaknesses and imperfections of their own faith, and they expressed a desire to possess greater faith.

> *The apostles said to the Lord, "Increase our faith [our ability to confidently trust in God and His power]." And the Lord said, "If you have [confident, abiding] faith in God [even as small] as a mustard seed, you could say to this mulberry tree [which has very strong roots], 'Be pulled up by the roots and be planted in the sea'; and [if the request was in agreement with the will of God] it would have obeyed you." – Luke 17:5-6 AMP*

"Jesus used this moment to emphasize to the disciples that a person's confident, abiding faith combined with God's power can produce amazing results, if the request is in harmony with

God's will. God is fully capable of doing that which man regards as impossible." – Amplified Bible; Footnote (b); Luke 17:6

In Mark chapter nine, we read about a desperate man who approached Jesus in need of a healing miracle for his son:

"Teacher, I brought my son so you could heal him. He is possessed by an evil spirit that won't let him talk. And whenever the spirit seizes him, it throws him violently on the ground. Then he foams at the mouth, grinds his teeth and becomes rigid." – Mark 9:17-18a NLT

The father was distressed over the condition of his son. His son had been tormented in this way since he was a little boy. The evil spirit often tried to kill his son by throwing him into the fire or the water. This heartbroken father pleaded with Jesus saying, "Have mercy on us and help us, if you can" (verse 22b NLT). Jesus replied to his request by saying, "If you can believe, all things are possible to him who believes" (verse 23 NKJV).

The difficulty at hand was not in Jesus's power or ability to heal but in this man's ability to believe. Recognizing his doubt and unbelief, the man began to weep. In all genuineness of heart, he cried out, "I do believe, but help me overcome my unbelief!" Jesus commanded the evil spirit to come out of the boy and never enter him again. He was healed, set free, and delivered (Mark 9:25). And we can be certain that this father began to experience a healing take place in his faith.

Sometimes faith and unbelief are found in the same heart. The disciples did, indeed, have faith, but their faith needed to be further developed. The father in Mark chapter nine had a measure of faith. However, he was having trouble believing for a miracle in the seemingly impossible circumstances of his son's long-time struggle. What parent cannot relate to being concerned or worried about their own child? Every believer may find himself at one time or another struggling with doubt or unbelief, especially in the storms of life. It is in times like these that we must put the faith that we do have, no matter how little it may seem to be at the time, into action, regardless of the circumstances. Never forget that there is an energizing force at work in you, Friend!

Now faith brings our hopes into reality and becomes the foundation needed to acquire the things we long for. It is all the evidence required to prove what is still unseen. This testimony of faith is what previous generations were commended for. Faith empowers us to see that the universe was created and beautifully coordinated by the power of God's words! He spoke and the invisible realm gave birth to all that is seen. – Hebrews 11:1-3 TPT

 **PRAYER**

Lord, I thank You that You are the miracle-working God. Nothing is too difficult for You. Today, I recognize the need for my own faith to continually be developed. Help me to press in when my faith is being tested. May I draw nearer to You during times like these and come to know You in greater ways. May I speak faith-filled words out of my mouth even when my heart feels as though it is wavering. May I continue to exercise my faith in the midst of trying times. Thank You, Jesus, for giving me opportunities to apply it. Deepen my trust. Lord, increase my faith. I desire to walk in an unswerving, confident, and abiding faith!

Therefore as you have received Christ Jesus the Lord, walk in [union with] Him [reflecting His character in the things you do and say—living lives that lead others away from sin], having been deeply rooted [in Him] and now being continually built up in Him and [becoming increasingly more] established in your faith. – Colossians 2:6-7a AMP

Moving from Worry to Faith

The fundamental fact of existence is that this trust in God, this faith, is the firm foundation under everything that makes life worth living. It's our handle on what we can't see. The act of faith is what distinguished our ancestors, set them above the crowd.

– Hebrews 11:1-2 MSG

Faith in God is the firm foundation under everything that makes life worth living! Therefore, it's time for us to move from the place of doubt to the place of faith. It's time for us to move from the place of worry, anxiety, and fear to the place of really trusting Jesus with our very lives. Doubt, worry, anxiety, and fear rob us from truly living an abundant life. In Mark chapter four verses eighteen and nineteen, we see how worry chokes the Word of God in our lives, making it unfruitful and barren. Worry sucks the very life right out of our faith. Worrying does not add one day to our lives. Instead, it subtracts from us, suffocating any potential growth. Doubt, worry, anxiety, and fear rob us of our peace, our happiness, and our joy. They compromise our overall well-being.

The Over-anxieties of Life

Henry Allon once spoke about the over-anxieties of life, describing them as "a restless, wearing, fretting anxiety, that cannot let us do our best, and then leave issues in the hands of God's providence." Allon was talking about being consumed with the cares of the world. He went on to say that when we allow ourselves to sink into this state of over-anxiety, "we give way to despondency; every experience seems a presage of evil, every road tangled and rough; we receive no gift of God with joy, we offer no prayer with thanksgiving; we fret ourselves, and perhaps charge God foolishly." I would add that the person consumed with the cares of life quickly loses their perspective. This kind of worrying is a form of doubt and unbelief. We must guard ourselves against it before it becomes sin before the Lord. When does normal concern and care become excessive?

> "The legitimate measure of even lawful care is exceeded when religious trust in God is disabled; when our spirit is so disquieted and absorbed that we cannot pray, save in the utterance of imperious desires; when the care intrudes at all times and overpowers all feelings, so that we cannot leave the issues with God. Undue care is one of the most inveterate forms of unbelief. It wears out physical energies, takes the vital spirit out of man; instead of a sound mind in a healthy body, he has to contend with a disordered mind in a body nervously unstrung; he can neither work by day nor sleep by night; full of morbid activity, he does nothing; his over-anxiety has defeated itself." – Henry Allon

Undue care and over-anxiety overwhelm the heart and hinder our prayer life. James chapter one tells us that the person in this condition is like a "wave of the sea driven and tossed by the wind." The experience of the individual is compared to being tossed about on the rough seas—up one minute and down the next. The Message Bible puts it like this:

> People who "worry their prayers" are like wind-whipped waves. Don't think you're going to get anything from the Master that way, adrift at sea, keeping all your options open. – James 1:7-8 MSG

"Keeping all your options open" isn't faith at all, is it? God wants us to be confident in Him and His Word. And He wants us to pray from the place of truly trusting Him.

> *But let him ask in faith, with no doubting, for he who doubts is like a wave of the sea driven and tossed by the wind. For let not that man suppose that he will receive anything from the Lord; he is a double-minded man, unstable in all his ways. – James 1:6-8 NKJV*

Double-minded and Unstable

A double-minded believer is always wavering in his heart between faith and unbelief. This creates such a restlessness within the mind and heart. James chapter one and verse eight says that this person becomes unstable in respect to everything! The word "ways" in the original Greek language is the word *hodos* and it means "on the road he is traveling or his journey." Metaphorically speaking, the term "in all his ways" means "in his course of conduct;" "his way of thinking, feeling, deciding;" and "in his progress." There is no stability in worrying! This unstable way of life distracts us from really living. And it hinders our spiritual growth. In Luke chapter twelve, Jesus addressed worrying about even our basic needs and provisions.

> *If God can clothe the fields and meadows with grass and flowers, can he not clothe you as well, O struggling one with so many doubts? I repeat: Don't let worry enter your life. Live above the anxious cares about your personal needs. – Luke 12:28-29 TPT*

Peace that Passes Understanding

There are many, many things that we could become burdened with. It's true. But Jesus longs to lift our burdens. It's not God's will for us to be filled with doubt, worry, anxiety, and fear but, rather, to be filled with His glorious peace and rest. We can, indeed, live above anxious cares through the power of Jesus Christ. Prayer is the remedy. Praying and choosing to trust God are steps in putting our faith into action.

> *Do not be anxious or worried about anything, but in everything [every circumstance and situation] by prayer and petition with thanksgiving, continue to make your [specific] requests known to God. And the peace of God [that peace that reassures the heart, that peace] which transcends all understanding [that peace which] stands guard over your hearts and your minds in Christ Jesus [is yours]. – Philippians 4:6-7 AMP*

If over-anxiety is the place where you have been living, it's time to move to a new address. Let's begin to rise above it, beginning today! Believe God concerning that situation, whatever it might be. Put it in His hands and leave it there. Do not let your heart be touched by fear or uncertainty. Pray to your heavenly Father. Cast all your cares upon Him, for He cares for you (1 Peter 5:7).

> *If you don't know what you're doing, pray to the Father. He loves to help. You'll get his help, and won't be condescended to when you ask for it. Ask boldly, believingly, without a second thought. – James 1:5-6 MSG*

This is where we want to live! It's that place of taking our cares to the Father, trusting Him without a second thought, and walking in the peace of God. We can have peace. Peace is ours! It's the kind of peace that settles in our hearts whether we see immediate changes or not. We can have this peace when circumstances are so intense that it doesn't even make sense to experience peace. It is inward peace under all events. It is a deep and constant peace. And it's an abiding peace that cannot be disturbed. The word peace in Philippians 4:7 translates as "rest, quietness, a state of tranquility, safety, and to be set at one again." What do you need today? Pray and release it to the Lord. And then receive His perfect peace.

Be carefree in the care of God! – Luke 12:24b TPT

 **PRAYER**

Lord Jesus, there is no room in my life for worry, anxiety, and fear. I will bring everything to you in prayer and leave it there in Your hands. I cast my cares upon You, for You care for me. I choose to live above every anxious care. Give me a stable mind, Lord. Cause me to become stable in my heart, thoughts, emotions, decisions, and in all my progress. I repent of any doubt and unbelief that has been hidden in my heart. Add back to me, Lord, any inward peace, happiness, and joy that has been subtracted from me. Cause me to grow in every area and bring forth good fruit. I desire to walk in the abundant life that You have made possible for all believers. My faith is the firm foundation under everything that makes my life worth living. Therefore, I will rest in You!

Don't fret or worry, instead of worrying, pray. Let petitions and praises shape your worries into prayers, letting God know your concerns. Before you know it, a sense of God's wholeness, everything coming together for good, will come and settle you down. It's wonderful what happens when Christ displaces worry at the center of your life. – Philippians 4:6-7 MSG

Cling to the Lord and Hold Fast

Trust in the Lord with all your heart, and lean not on your own understanding; in all your ways acknowledge Him, and He shall direct your paths.

– Proverbs 3:5-6 NKJV

Trusting in the Lord brings sweet peace and rest to the inner heart and life. The more we trust Him the more peace and rest we experience. Proverbs 3:5 tells us to trust the Lord with our whole heart! To trust God is to rely on Him. Webster's definition of trust is a resting of the mind on the integrity, veracity, justice, friendship, and sound principles of another person. Surely, we can put our confidence in the person of Jesus Christ. Most certainly, He is worthy of our trust. Trusting is also defined as committing something to a person's care, use, or management. Isn't that what we are really doing when we give our lives to Christ? The word "trust" in Proverbs 3:5 is the word *batach* in the original Hebrew language, and while it simply means to rely upon and have confidence in the Lord, it also means to cling to and hold fast to Him. In addition, this word *batach* (trust) means to feel safe. Does your heart feel safe today? The key to having and maintaining this trust and safety is found in verse six: "In all your ways acknowledge Him."

Life-giving Intimacy

The word "acknowledge" is the Hebrew word *yada,* and it is important to note because it literally translates as "to discover and know personally." It refers to life-giving intimacy. It suggests direct, intimate contact with God along with prayer that conceives and births blessings and victories! It's all about our relationship with God. To know Him more is to trust Him more! And we are to acknowledge him in all our ways, on every road we are traveling. It is our life journey, wherever it may take us and whatever we may face along the way. It's time to acknowledge Him in every situation. He's there. He's present. He's a friend that sticks closer than a brother. Recognize His presence and activity in every part of your life. Acknowledge Him in every joy and in every sorrow. Cling to Him in times of distress, anguish, and uncertainty. Hold fast to Him in the midst of life's storms. He is the Lord over sickness, disease, spiritual forces of darkness, and even nature itself. Acknowledge His power and His authority when faced with seemingly impossible situations. He is the God who is able to do exceedingly, abundantly more than you can ever ask or imagine (Eph 3:20-21). So go ahead and acknowledge Him in the midst of every hurt and disappointment. Acknowledge Him when things seem unfair. And acknowledge Him right in the midst of your loneliness. Put your confidence in Jesus. Trust and believe! If we will maintain our life-giving intimacy with the Lord, our trust will be ever deepened.

We must always keep God in our view and look for His direction. We will most certainly come up against things that we cannot control, change, or fix. We will need to seek the Lord for answers and direction. There will be times in our lives when we just will not see a way to victory. The answers will simply be out of our own human reach, strength, and resources. After all, our understanding is limited. Our knowledge is limited. Our own ability is limited. In times like these, the Word of God instructs us to trust the Lord with our whole heart and acknowledge Him. We must steady our hearts and press in toward the Lord.

Don't be pulled in different directions or worried about a thing. Be saturated in prayer throughout each day, offering your faith-filled requests before God with overflowing gratitude. Tell him every detail of your life. – Philippians 4:6 TPT

That is a life of daily, habitual prayer and continual communion with God. Do not wait until you're in a crisis. Always keep the line of communication open. Draw near to God, and He will draw near to you.

Trust the Lord completely, and do not rely on your own opinions. With all your heart rely on him to guide you, and he will lead you in every decision you make. Become intimate with him in whatever you do, and he will lead you wherever you go. Don't think for a moment that you know it all, for wisdom comes when you adore him with undivided devotion and avoid everything that's wrong. Then you will find healing refreshment your body and spirit long for. – Proverbs 3:5-8 TPT

Healing Refreshment

Healing refreshment is the byproduct of trusting the Lord as you maintain an intimate relationship with Him, adoring Him with undivided devotion. And wisdom comes from that place of relationship with the Lord!

We cannot lean on our own understanding. Man's wisdom is insufficient. True wisdom comes from the Lord. Oh, how we need His wisdom. Proverbs 3:13 says, "Happy is the man who finds wisdom, and the man who gains understanding." The Bible refers to the understanding that comes from the Lord as "living-understanding." The Amplified Bible puts it like this:

Happy [blessed, considered fortunate, to be admired] is the man who finds [skillful and godly] wisdom, and the man who gains understanding and insight [learning from God's word and life's experiences]. – Proverbs 3:13 AMP

He is the All-Wise, All-knowing God, the Creator of man and the universe. He is the Author and Finisher of our faith. We need Him to impart wisdom and living understanding to us.

Blessings pour over the ones who find wisdom, for they have obtained living understanding. As wisdom increases, a great treasure is imparted, greater than many bars of refined gold. It is a more valuable commodity than gold and gemstones, for there is nothing you desire that could compare to her. Wisdom extends to you long life in one hand and wealth and promotion in the other. Out of her mouth flows righteousness, and her words release both law and mercy. The ways of wisdom are sweet, always drawing you into the place of wholeness. Seeking for her brings the discovery of untold blessings, for she is the healing tree of life to those who taste her fruits. – Proverbs 3:13-18 TPT

My child, never drift off course from these two goals for your life: to walk in wisdom and to discover your purpose. Don't ever forget how they empower you. For they strengthen you inside and out and inspire you to do what's right; you will be energized and refreshed by the healing they bring. They give you living hope to guide you, and not one of life's tests will cause you to stumble. You will sleep like a baby, safe and sound— your rest will be sweet and secure. You will not be subject to terror, for it will not terrify you. Nor will the disrespectful be able to push you aside, because God is your confidence in times of crisis, keeping your heart at rest in every situation. – Proverbs 3:21-26 TPT

When we gain wisdom from Him, we have the tools we need for understanding the proper way to live. Blessings flow like a fountain. Wisdom that comes from the Lord is more valuable than anything else one can obtain. It brings with it long life, wholeness, and healing refreshment. The believer is strengthened inside and out. He is energized. The Christian believer is filled with a sense of inner rest, peace, safety, security, and hope! Is there any reason you would not choose to trust in the Lord with your whole heart? Do not withhold any part of your heart from Him, for He is not withholding any part of His heart from you.

Scholars tell us that the word "trust" has a graphic, pictorial meaning and signifies literally to cling to or hold fast to God. It expresses the notion of a good tight grip upon Him as well as intimate union with Him.

> "That is faith, cleaving to Christ, turning round Him with all the tendrils of our heart, as the vine does round its pole, holding to Him by His hand, as a tottering man does by the strong hand that upholds." – Alexander Maclaren

PRAYER

Lord, I trust You with all of my heart. I acknowledge Your power and authority over all things. You are sovereign, Lord, and I bless You. I acknowledge Your work throughout my life. I commit my life to Your care and management, for You are worthy. You are my confidence. My eyes are fixed on You. My heart clings to You. I adore you with undivided devotion. As I draw near to You, Lord, impart Your wisdom and living understanding to me. In Jesus's name!

How happy is the man who trusts in Him! – Psalm 34:8b NLV

Adapt

For it is not from man that we draw our life but from God as we are being joined to Jesus, the Anointed One. And now he is our God-given wisdom, our virtue, our holiness, and our redemption.

– 1 Corinthians 1:30 TPT

We draw our life from God! You and I have everything we need when we are joined to Christ. He gives us the power and ability to overcome life's challenges. We grow and flourish in spite of them. It's God's purpose that we thrive in every season of our lives. We must become resilient and learn to adapt throughout life's changes. Look at all of creation! In Scripture, we have repeatedly been compared to trees, flourishing plants, and verdant green leaves. These plants adapt to their environment in a way that assures their continued growth. They adapt in order to flourish and thrive even in the midst of unfavorable circumstances. If God, the creator of all things, put the ability to adapt and thrive within the plants of the earth, surely He has placed an even greater capacity within you and me, having been created in His very image!

Learning to Adapt

What exactly does it mean to adapt? To adapt means to become adjusted to new conditions. Adapting means to make suitable for a new purpose. It is to modify, adjust, readjust, rework, or make work. To adapt is to acclimate oneself, to come to terms with, to get one's bearings, and to find one's feet again. The faster we learn to adapt, the quicker we can begin to experience happiness and begin to really live.

Throughout the Bible, God points us to nature to teach us important truths. What can we learn from His creation that we can apply to our own lives? Let's explore!

Lessons from Nature

When it comes to a deciduous tree, the fluid that flows through it is thin and susceptible to freezing. The tree's tissue is tender, so it saves energy by shedding its leaves. The season begins to change from fall to winter, and the tree senses a loss of daylight. It begins to go through a chemical change. The plant's leaves fall to the ground, but even what it sheds serves a purpose and has a role to play in its success. The leaves that the tree has lost fall to the ground, decompose, and their nutrients trickle back into the soil. These nutrients then begin nourishing the tree. What appears to be a loss becomes fertilizer.

An evergreen, on the other hand, can hang onto its leaves all winter long because it is coated with a waxy substance that protects it against freezing cold, harsh temperatures. Its cells produce an antifreeze-type chemical that protects it from the worst of the winter season. The tree continues to thrive in spite of the harsh elements. And then there are some plants, like the cactus plant for example, that can thrive in hot, dry environments. These plants have an extensive root system that spreads out and goes deep. A cactus can reduce water loss by storing water in its stem or body to survive the infrequent rainfall. It stores water in between periods of rainfall to be used for continued growth. It adapts! It is truly amazing that cacti can survive in such parched places almost against all odds. Yet they do survive, and they flourish, producing beautiful, vibrant flowers.

Because plants are typically held in place by soil, they cannot move around. They cannot just pick up and move from one environment to another. Plants cannot get away from those outside elements and factors that are compromising their health, growth, and livelihood. So, the plant's way of responding to its less-than-ideal environment is by changing how it grows. One way that a plant responds is by turning or bending in a certain way. The plant has special cells in the tips of its roots that can detect small changes in gravity. And it responds to the changes that it senses. If you turn a plant on its side, the plant's roots will start to grow downward. You may have seen this before. No matter what changes the plant experiences within its environment, it will thrive because of its root system. It is dependent upon that root system!

A plant also responds to changes in light. Plant stems and leaves grow in the direction of the light. A plant can detect the daily cycle of light and darkness. Some plants open their leaves during the day, collecting light. Then the plant closes its leaves at night to protect it from water loss. Some flowers close their petals at night as a defense mechanism that the plant has developed to preserve its pollen. By closing at night, it is protecting itself from the elements that may otherwise compromise its livelihood: wind, dew, rain, and such. The plant's response assures that the pollinating insects can do their job more efficiently in the daytime. The flowers close themselves off to the darkness to protect their growth and vitality.

Plants are also affected by disease much like we are. Typically, their first line of defense is death to the diseased-ridden part of the plant. We prune our plants when we see those dead, diseased, or unproductive parts, don't we? Sometimes we trim them to bring them to a flourishing state. We do this so they will become healthy again so they will grow and flourish even more. It's our attempt to save them. Much in the same way, a plant will stop feeding the parts that may compromise the entire plant itself. Many plants also produce special chemicals to fight disease. Willow trees, for example, produce a chemical that kills bacteria. Some of those same compounds, like salicylic acid, are used in our acne products.

Many plants can survive in extreme places, such as rocky mountain tops where the soil is shallow, alkaline, and deficient in nutrients.

They adapt to store food, moisture, and energy during fluctuating temperatures and elements. Strong direct sun, arid seasons, freezing-low temperatures, harsh winds, snow-packed winters, oxygen-deficient atmospheres, and the like compromise their ability to support and sustain their very life. Nevertheless, they adapt in many ways, such as growing closer to the ground, producing smaller leaves to prevent water loss, and growing long taproots. Other plants survive in the marshy wetlands where the soil is thin and acidic. The nutrients are washed from the soil because of the constantly wet conditions. And yet, plants will not only survive in these environments, but they will also thrive as they adapt. Most are carnivorous plants like the Venus flytrap, for example. The Venus flytrap will, as the name suggests, trap and digest insects and other small animals to get most of its nutrients. This plant and others find a way to nourish in order to flourish. This ability to adapt cuts through, works around, and crosses over every disadvantage.

Plants like these mentioned, and many others, have developed special traits to help them survive and thrive in diverse places. Diverse places, unfavorable environments, extreme conditions. . . Many of us have already spent much of our lives contending with the same. However, I wonder how much of our lives have been spent in surviving mode rather than thriving mode. It is not God's purpose that we merely survive—just making it through another day, another week, or another year. Jesus came that we might have an abundant life—a full, meaningful life. One that is worth living. Second Peter chapter one and verse three tells us that God has given us all things pertaining to life and godliness. He is our life-giver, and He knows how to equip us with just what we need, just when we need it!

How are we doing when it comes to our ability to adapt in all circumstances? I'm not talking about putting up with things we shouldn't be putting up with. I am talking about thriving in the midst of changes that take place in our lives, the kind of changes that catapult us into places that we never dreamed or imagined we would find ourselves in. I'm talking about navigating through the kind of events that take place in our lives that were not planned, anticipated, or welcomed. During those times when we feel like the rug has been pulled out from underneath us, can we adapt in a way that assures our entire world is not rocked? Can we roll with the tide in a way that assures steady growth? Can we continue to flourish and thrive without a hitch? The truth is that we can. We can develop these traits. Let's enter into the most intimate relationship with Jesus, draw our life from Him, and become the resilient, thriving believers that He has created us the be!

Resilient – able to withstand or recover quickly from difficult conditions, tending to recover from or adjust easily to misfortune or change, springing back; rebounding, returning to the original form or position after being bent, compressed, or stretched, able to be happy, successful, again after something difficult or bad has happened.

> *His divine power has given to us all things that pertain to life and godliness, through the knowledge of Him who called us by glory and virtue, by which have been given to us exceedingly great and precious promises, that through these you may be partakers of the divine nature, having escaped the corruption that is in the world through lust. – 2 Peter 1:3-4 NKJV*

 **PRAYER**

Thank You, Lord, that You have placed the ability within me to adapt in all circumstances. You have deposited within me everything I need for life and godliness. I am more than an overcomer through the power of Jesus Christ. Even my losses are turned to gain. You turn every disadvantage I encounter into an advantage for my overall good. I bounce back from every setback and recover all. I am resilient. My roots go deep. I draw my life from You. I don't merely survive, but I thrive. And I give You glory, for You make me strong.

Everything we could ever need for life and godliness has already been deposited in us by his divine power. For all this was lavished upon us through the rich experience of knowing him who has called us by name and invited us to come to him through a glorious manifestation of his goodness. As a result of this, he has given you magnificent promises that are beyond all price, so that through the power of these tremendous promises we can experience partnership with the divine nature, by which you have escaped the corrupt desires that are of the world. – 2 Peter 1:3-4 TPT

Walking in Wisdom

To everything there is a season, a time for every purpose under heaven; a time to be born, and a time to die; a time to plant, and a time to pluck what is planted; a time to kill, and a time to heal; a time to break down, and a time to build up; a time to weep, and a time to laugh; a time to mourn, and a time to dance; a time to cast away stones, and a time to gather stones, a time to embrace, and a time to refrain from embracing; a time to gain, and a time to lose; a time to keep, and a time to throw away; a time to tear, and a time to repair; a time to keep silent, and a time to speak; a time to love, and a time to hate; a time of war and a time of peace.

– Ecclesiastes 3:1-8 NKJV

Jesus is our center. We draw life from Him. He gives us strength and empowers us to thrive in every season of our lives. Ecclesiastes 3:1-8 describes many different seasons and emotions we face within our lifetime. Many seasons are difficult seasons. And the changes that come with them are downright hard! *The Pulpit Commentary* says, "Our faculties and capacities are many, our experiences are varied, for the appeals made to us by our environment change from day to day, from hour to hour." It goes on to describe the changing of seasons as "a constant ebbing and flowing, waxing and waning, from one extreme to another." How do we navigate through these changes successfully? How do we move right through extremes in a way that does not throw us off course? We learn to adapt, and we become resilient. We also develop wisdom, not man's wisdom but the wisdom of God.

"Wisdom gives the ability to take raw facts and draw right conclusions." – The Passion Translation; Footnote (a); Proverbs 3:13

Drawing the wrong conclusions or even jumping to conclusions can have a negative impact on our mental and emotional health and our overall well-being. It can set us off in the wrong direction with the wrong mentality, the wrong actions, and the wrong consequences. Are you able to draw the right conclusions in the midst of sudden changes and distress?

My child, never drift off course from these two goals for your life: to walk in wisdom and to discover your purpose. Don't ever forget how they empower you. For they strengthen you inside and out and inspire you to do what's right; you will be energized and refreshed by the healing they bring. – Proverbs 3:21-22 TPT

Walking in wisdom and discovering your purpose empowers you, strengthens you, and inspires you. Solomon, the writer of both Proverbs and Ecclesiastes, did drift off course. In fact, he drifted off course from both goals at different times in his life. It was such a shame, too. After all, Solomon was handed an opportunity of a lifetime when God said to him, "Ask! What shall I give you?" in 2 Chronicles 1:6-7. Solomon replied that he wanted wisdom and knowledge to rule his kingdom well and to make good decisions for his people. God was pleased with his answer. Because he did not ask for things like riches, wealth, honor, long life, or revenge against his enemies, God granted Solomon's request. And not only did God give Solomon wisdom, but He added all those other things to him also. Solomon's reign began under the greatest advantage and most promising future ever. He had everything he needed to thrive under every circumstance imaginable, but soon afterward, Solomon's own wisdom alone began guiding him. Consequently, it wasn't long before Solomon lost all sense of purpose in his life. How did it happen? How did he move so far away from the purposes of God?

Solomon took many wives, including pagan wives, against God's counsel. Then he began tolerating their idolatry and sinful practices. Later, he began practicing idolatry himself. And Solomon set out on a quest to find happiness apart from God. Soon, he was searching for meaning and purpose in his life. In Ecclesiastes chapter two, Solomon recounts how he built houses, planted vineyards, cultivated gardens, established orchards, and constructed water pools. He acquired servants, possessions, herds, and flocks, more so than anyone else in Jerusalem. He gathered silver, gold, and special treasures of kings and provinces. Solomon purchased singers and entertainers. He gratified his flesh with alcohol, parties, and women. The Word of God tells us that whatever Solomon's heart desired he did not withhold from himself. Everything he wanted he took. Solomon never said no to himself. He gave in to every impulse. Solomon had wealth and influence. He had resources and power. King Solomon had everything anyone could ever want. He even became educated beyond all others in his kingdom. It was man's wisdom and knowledge that he had gained, however. The Amplified Bible uses the words "human wisdom and experience." Solomon attained greatness in the world's eyes (Ecclesiastes chapters 1 and 2).

King Solomon had seen it all and done it all. However, the thrill and happiness all these things brought into his life were short-lived. The satisfaction was temporary. And he was left feeling empty, unfulfilled, and without purpose. In Ecclesiastes chapter two and verse seventeen, Solomon actually said that he hated his life! It was distressing to him. All his striving brought him to despair. He even stated that he had come to hate the very things his labor had provided for him. He reasoned that man's labor, the chasing after and striving for things, left man sorrowful. It was burdensome, leaving people with no rest. After all of Solomon's seeking and searching, he came to some pretty solid conclusions. All this chasing and striving was vanity, full of emptiness and dissatisfaction. All this work to acquire material things, it was absurdity, futility—full of frustration and nonsense. Finding real happiness and satisfaction within material things, pleasures, and relationships was like grasping for the wind. In Ecclesiastes chapter one and verse eight, Solomon said, "Everything is boring, utterly boring— no one can find any meaning in it" (MSG). Imagine having everything you thought you ever wanted and being bored with it all! Solomon had everything and yet he had nothing.

> *Then I looked on all the works that my hands had done and on the labor in which I had toiled; and indeed all was vanity and grasping for the wind. There was no profit under the sun. – Ecclesiastes 2:11 NKJV*

It was all pointless. Finding happiness and real value in life apart from God was an illusion. Solomon realized that all men—rich and poor, great and small, highly intelligent and completely uneducated alike— will all die at the end of their lives. They cannot take any of their wealth, pleasures, or greatness with them. Solomon took a good, hard look at it all—how he was living and all the things he had been chasing after. Everything he had done up until this point was all done without God's guidance. And every road he traveled in pursuit of happiness led to a dead end. Finally, he returned to God. He returned to seeking God and being led by Him. He returned to trusting the Lord and following His guidance. The wisdom of God began unfolding in his life. Solomon was able to arrive at the right conclusions that finally set him on the right path up until old age.

Sometimes, you have to stop and reevaluate some things: where you've been, where you are right now, and the direction you might be headed in. *The Sermon Bible Commentary* says that you are "not to be deceived by any suggestion of the human heart which would lead you to fancy that God's precepts are not wise, and that you can find happiness in any ways which are not the ways of holiness." Instead, you are to "hold fast to the best conclusion which true wisdom furnishes – namely, the conviction that it must be a vain search to look for happiness in any way but this."

In Matthew 6:33, Jesus tells us to seek first the kingdom of God and His righteousness, and all these other things will be added to us. God's kingdom is His rule, His realm, and His will. *Thayer's Greek-English Lexicon of the New Testament* defines His righteousness as integrity, virtue, purity of life, and correctness of thinking, feeling, and acting. It is the right state of the heart with reference to heavenly and earthly things. We must make the things of God the object of our first choice, seeking them before anything else.

> *So above all, constantly seek God's kingdom and his righteousness, then all these less important things will be given to you abundantly. –* Matthew 6:33 TPT

J. Vaughan says that "the season of all the disappointment and all the unhappiness which there is in this world is, that that great precept of order is not kept." You see, whatever we place first in our hearts and whatever we consider of greatest importance in our lives will have an impact on what we chase and how much lasting happiness we enjoy.

Where has your own searching led you? What has been the pursuit of your heart? Are you following this great precept of order, or have you been chasing less important things? Have you drifted off course?

There is a season and a time for everything under the sun, Friend. And it is my conclusion that the time has come for us to be happy, fulfilled, satisfied, and full of purpose! It is time to chase after the Lord and remember that His Word tells us that He, Himself, is our satisfaction, our portion, and our very great reward. May Christ, and your relationship with Him become your true passion.

> *What joy overwhelms everyone who keeps the ways of God, those who seek him as their heart's passion! –* Psalm 119:2 TPT

> *You are my satisfaction, Lord, and all that I need, so I'm determined to do everything you say. –* Psalm 119:57 TPT

> *My flesh and my heart fail; but God is the strength of my heart and my portion forever. –* Psalm 73:26 NKJV

I am your shield, your exceedingly great reward. – Genesis 15:1b NKJV

 **PRAYER**

Jesus, You are my center. My main pursuit is knowing You and experiencing a close, intimate relationship with You. There is nothing I desire more than You. I will give you first place in my heart, for You are my passion. All that I need is found in the person of Jesus Christ. As I seek You and set my gaze upon You, help me to walk in wisdom every day of my life. Help me to discover my true purpose. Empower me, strengthen me, and inspire me. Energize, refresh, and heal me. You are truly the strength of my heart, my portion forever, and my very great reward. Praise be to the name of the Lord! Blessed be Your name.

Happy is the man who finds wisdom, and the man who gains understanding. – Proverbs 3:13 NKJV

Finding Purpose

To everything there is a season, a time for every purpose under heaven; a time to be born, and a time to die; a time to plant, and a time to pluck what is planted; a time to kill, and a time to heal; a time to break down, and a time to build up; a time to weep, and a time to laugh; a time to mourn, and a time to dance; a time to cast away stones, and a time to gather stones, a time to embrace, and a time to refrain from embracing; a time to gain, and a time to lose; a time to keep, and a time to throw away; a time to tear, and a time to repair; a time to keep silent, and a time to speak; a time to love, and a time to hate; a time of war, and a time of peace.

— Ecclesiastes 3:1-8 NKJV

Ecclesiastes chapter three tells us that there is a season and time for everything and that every season is full of God's purposes. The seasons presented first in this passage are the time of birth and the time of death. In the following verses, we find many of the events and emotions that take place in between. These are events that are common to all people. And they should not take us by surprise.

"The seasons are a perpetual procession, and endless chain, an ever-moving wheel. Cold flies before heat, and anon summer is chased away by winter. Nothing is stable. Such is life: such are the feelings of spiritual life with most men; such is the history of the church of God. We sorrow and we rejoice: we struggle, and we triumph: we labor and we rest. We are not long upon Tabor, neither are we always in the valley of Baca. Let us not be amazed, as though some strange thing happened to us, if our day darkens into night, or our summer chills into winter. From joy to sorrow, from sorrow to joy, from success to defeat, from defeat to success, we pass very rapidly. It is so: it will be so while the earth remaineth, and we remain partakers of the earth." – Charles Spurgeon

We must expect change rather than be discouraged by it. It is not God's purpose that we live empty, tired, and defeated lives. It is not His will for us to slip into a miserable state when faced with unwelcomed change or difficulties. Our lives should be so full and so rich no matter what circumstances we face and no matter what season of life we happen to be in. However, if we are going to be victorious and thrive in every season of our lives, we are going to need to know a few things. Just as there is a time to lose, a time to mourn, and a time to weep, there is also a time to gain, a time to rejoice, and a time to laugh. There is a time to speak, a time to let go of the past, and a time to move forward. There is a time to heal, a time to repair, and a time to build. And there is also a time to reap a good harvest!

> For everything there is **a season**, and a time. – Ecclesiastes 3:1a ESV (Emphasis added)

The word "season" in Ecclesiastes 3:1 is the word *ze man* in the original Hebrew language, and it means "an opportune time" and "an appointed time." It is an appointed time in that it was decided beforehand just for you. It is an appointed time in that it has an appointed beginning, an appointed duration, and an appointed end. Seasons don't last forever. They come and they go. Seasons change. And if it is a particularly difficult season, it helps to remember that! This too shall pass.

For everything there is a season, and ***a time****. – Ecclesiastes 3:1a ESV (Emphasis added)*

The word "time" translates as "a right time" and "especially now." You can be sure that the season that you are in right now is filled with great purpose. Within each season of our lives (whether grand, bland, or downright painful), purpose exists. Our goal is to recognize it and partner with the Lord in accomplishing His purposes. Don't fight your season. Embrace it. And find purpose.

He has made everything beautiful in its time. – Ecclesiastes 3:11a AMPC

God is making everything beautiful in its time! It may not always look like anything beautiful is happening in a particular season of our lives. You may be walking through a season filled with many burdens as you read these words today, but God will, indeed, make all things beautiful. And we can believe that truth no matter what our circumstances presently look like! In Ecclesiastes 3:10-11, Solomon said that he had seen the burdens people face in their lives, but nevertheless, God is making everything beautiful!

Nevertheless

I have seen the burden God has placed on us all. Yet God has made everything beautiful for its own time. He has planted eternity in the human heart, but even so, people cannot see the whole scope of God's work from beginning to end. – Ecclesiastes 10-11 NLT

We do not see the whole picture of what God is doing in our lives, and therefore, we often judge things incorrectly. We jump to the wrong conclusions. Adam Clark says, "We must wait with patience the full discovery of that which seems intricate and perplexed, acknowledging that we cannot find out the work that God makes from beginning to end, and therefore must judge nothing before the time. We are to believe that God has made all things beautiful. Everything is done well, as in creation, so in providence, and we shall see it when the end comes, but till then we are incomplete judges of it."

How have you been judging your present situation? Be careful, Friend.

> *He has made everything beautiful in its time. He has also planted eternity in men's hearts and minds (a divinely implanted sense of purpose working through the ages) which nothing under the sun but God can satisfy. – Ecclesiastes 3:11 AMPC*

Have you had a sense of purpose in your heart for where you are walking right now? Seek the Lord for His purpose.

When it comes to true, lasting happiness, the reality is that it just does not matter what these circumstances are in your present situation. It's not life's circumstances that bring us satisfaction. We tend to forget that sometimes. True satisfaction comes from the Lord. We cannot look to our spouse to bring that satisfaction. We cannot look to our children to bring that satisfaction. It is not found in our careers, material possessions, or relationships with family, friends, or lovers. There is nothing under the sun but God who can truly satisfy.

> *Wherefore I **perceive** that there is nothing better, than that a man should rejoice in his own works; for that is his portion. – Ecclesiastes 3:22a KJV (Emphasis added)*

What is in your hands right now? How have you been viewing your daily activities and responsibilities? The word "perceive" in Ecclesiastes chapter three and verse twenty-two means "to regard with respect and to look upon with joy." Your portion, your lot, is what God has blessed you with right now. There is nothing better for you to do than rejoice in that! Verse twenty-two could be interpreted like this: There is nothing better, greater, than for you to rejoice, take joy, cheer up, be glad in your present season, right now, for it is your portion and a gift. It is what God has blessed you with. Rejoice! Be thankful!

"Do not turn God's blessings into sin by complaining; make the best of it. God will sweeten its bitters to you, if you will be faithful...The evils of life may be so sanctified to you as to work for your good. Though even wretched without, you may be happy within; for God can make all grace abound towards you."
– Adam Clarke

God can make all grace abound toward you! Thank you, Jesus! We may not fully understand the things we walk through at times. We may be powerless to control the timing of the events that take place in our lives, but what we do have power over is how we respond. Will we continue to cling to God and trust Him in the midst of an uncertain future? Will we adapt and be resilient? Will we acknowledge God in all things and allow Him to mold us and shape us? Will we work with God in whatever purpose He may have for us in each season? Will we rejoice and be thankful?

*Wherefore I perceive that there is nothing better, than that a man should **rejoice** in his own works; for that is his portion. – Ecclesiastes 3:22a KJV (Emphasis added)*

The word "rejoice" in verse twenty-two translates as "calm delight." We are to walk with an overall sense of calm delight, whether we are experiencing a winter season, a spring season, a summer season, or a fall season, knowing that God will make all things beautiful. He is landscaping our lives like a vibrant, flourishing, and thriving salvation garden. Let's allow God, our Gardener, to do His work. Perhaps Charles Spurgeon's thoughts on the seasons of our lives can lend us a fresh perspective today that we can carry forward.

"So too have I seen in our mortal life summer and winter, prosperity and adversity. Do not expect, dear brothers and sisters, while you are in this world, always to dwell among the lilies and roses of prosperity. Summer will come, and you will be wise to make hay while the sun shines by using all opportunities for usefulness; but look for winter. I do not know into what trade you can enter to be secure against losses, nor what profession you could follow in which you would escape disappointments. I know of no corner of the earth without night, no land without its stones, no sea without its storms. As to spiritual and mental experience, it seemeth to me within myself that while the earth remaineth I shall have my ebbs and flows, my risings and my sinkings. Do not therefore begin to kick or quarrel with the dispensations of God's province. When it is summertime say, 'The Lord gave, and blessed be his name.' When it is winter say, 'The Lord hath taken away, and blessed be his name.' Keep to the same music, even though you sometimes have to pitch an octave lower. Still praise and magnify the Lord whether you be sowing or reaping. Let him do what seemeth him good, but to you let it always seem good to praise." – Charles Spurgeon

Can you maintain your praise unto God through every season of your life? Can you maintain your inner peace and happiness no matter what comes and goes? The truth is that it is a choice. It's a decision! What will you decide?

Whatever happens, my dear brothers and sisters, rejoice in the Lord.
– Philippians 3:1a NLT

PRAYER

Lord, in every season of my life, let me be found giving praise unto You and magnifying Your great name. In the midst of difficulty, I will remember Your faithfulness. When I cannot see Your hand moving and working in my life, I will trust Your heart. I will stand on Your Word. Steady my heart. Help me to experience a sense of calm delight within my very soul even in times of uncertainty and trials. Thank You, Lord, for You make all grace abound toward me! You are writing the story of my life. You are filling the pages with good things. My story is not over yet! You are making all things beautiful in its time. Fill me, now, with a sense of great purpose and fulfill Your plan for me.

Be cheerful with joyous celebration in every season of life. Let joy overflow, for you are united with the Anointed One! – Philippians 4:4 TPT

Rejoice

Wherefore I perceive that there is nothing better, than that a man should rejoice in his own works; for that is his portion.

– Ecclesiastes 3:22 KJV

God has made everything beautiful in its time. He has planted a sense of purpose within each of us. We are to take joy in the works of our hands and our own activities in this season of our lives, but even those activities themselves will not fulfill that deep place of the inner man. That is the place that God has reserved for Himself alone to fill. When we seek God first, we find that we are satisfied in Him. Everything else in our lives becomes an added blessing. And when we understand these things, we are able to maintain our praise unto God in every season of our lives! We learn to adapt in a way that leaves us unscathed by the difficulties we face, and we continue to flourish just as God intended us to. We change the way we are growing like those plants that have to bend this way and that way. Many times, this bending is a bending of our own will. Refusing to be withered people of God, we turn away from darkness, cut off what's dead or diseased in our lives, store up the living Word of God within us, place our trust in Jesus, and depend on our root system. We begin to rejoice and regard our present activities with respect, and we look upon them with joy! We bend and we change the way we think about it. We rejoice and say, "Thank You, Lord, for this gift!"

Rejoice in the Lord always. Again I will say, rejoice! – Philippians 4:4 NKJV

Paul approached everything in his life as a gift. And when Paul wrote these words in Philippians chapter four, he was a prisoner in Rome. Under afflictions, distress, and persecution, he maintained his praise unto God. And he called on his readers to rejoice in the Lord always. "Always" means "at all times." That includes times of trouble and chaos. It means even in the midst of the afflictions now distressing you. Paul truly led by example. You could say that Paul was an expert and an authority on the subject, and he spoke these words with true authority. The apostle who said that he had found the recipe for being happy left us the simple, plain, reliable, and foolproof ingredients!

Be cheerful with joyous celebration in every season of life. Let your joy overflow, for you are united with the Anointed One! Let gentleness be seen in every relationship, for our Lord is near. Don't be pulled in different directions or worried about a thing. Be saturated in prayer throughout each day, offering your faith-filled requests before God with overflowing gratitude. – Philippians 4:4-6a TPT

You see, no matter what Paul was facing, he knew how to rejoice and give thanks. He was content and continually happy because he was habitually thankful. It wasn't that Paul was happy about the circumstances taking place in his life, but rather, he was happy in the midst of them.

"There is a luminousness, and a joyfulness, and a habitual thanksgiving in Paul's life, which contrast very strangely with the outward facts and conditions of that life...He had been subjected to every indignity of body and soul that a man could undergo. And yet, in other words, he says, 'Let your disposition be such that you shall see so many things to give thanks for that whenever you have occasion to ask for anything you shall do it through the radiant atmosphere of thanksgiving for all the mercies by which you are surrounded.'" – H. W. Beecher

The Radiant Atmosphere of Thanksgiving

Oh, that you and I would create a radiant atmosphere of thanksgiving. The Lord is pleased with a heart that is grateful. This we know, but do we also realize that a grateful heart releases something within the believer as well? There is something about a grateful heart that brings forth happiness, contentment, and satisfaction! The word "thanksgiving" in Philippians chapter four is the word *eucharistia* in the original Greek language, and it translates as "gratitude, grateful language (to God, as an act of worship); thankfulness or the giving of thanks." Paul understood the significance of a grateful heart. And in Hebrews chapter twelve verse twenty-eight, Paul asks us if we, too, see the importance of a thankful heart:

> *Do you see how thankful we must be? Not only thankful, but brimming with worship, deeply reverent before God.* – *Hebrews 12:28b* MSG

In Colossians chapter two, gratitude is a given! It is the fruit of one's faith.

> *Having been deeply rooted [in Him] and now being continually built up in Him [becoming increasingly more] established in your faith, just as you were taught, and overflowing in it with gratitude.* – *Colossians 2:7* AMP

And here in Philippians chapter four, Paul tells us to rejoice. Be grateful. Give thanks. Count your blessings! It's so important. It's so central. It's so paramount that Paul says it not just once but twice!

> *Rejoice in the Lord always [delight, take pleasure in Him]; again I will say, rejoice!* – *Philippians 4:4* AMP

The word "rejoice" here is the word *chairo* in the original Greek language, and it means to be full of cheer, to be calmly happy, to be well, and to thrive! Paul delighted himself in the Lord. He rolled his anxious thoughts upon Jesus as he brought every care to the throne of God in prayer. And he continually gave thanks in all things. Truly, you and I have so many reasons to be thankful. When it comes to rejoicing, Albert Barnes says, "It is a privilege to do this, not at certain periods and at distant intervals, but at all times."

Begin to exercise this privilege every single day. Trusting God is a decision. Maintaining praise unto the Lord is a choice. Rejoicing and giving thanks are choices and decisions as well. Paul exhorts the believer to rejoice, take joy, gladden yourself, and be happy!

Abraham Lincoln once said, "People are just as happy as they make up their minds to be!" I don't know about you, but I have decided that come hell or high water, I will be happy in the Lord. I will fully live! What will your decision be?

> *I will bless the Lord at all times: his praise shall continually be in my mouth.* – Psalm 34:1 KJV

PRAYER

Lord, I rejoice right now in this present season of my life. I regard everything that is on my plate and in my hands with respect and look upon it with joy! I honor and respect all You have given me. I am blessed. I am grateful! Thank You, Lord. You bestow gift after gift after gift upon my life. And You do it daily. Moreover, I am satisfied with You! All praise and honor and glory be to the most high God. Continue to fill my life with good things. Help me to embrace all that You desire to accomplish in and through me, even when things don't look quite like I thought they would. I will choose to trust You. I will bless Your name at all times. Your praise shall be continually on my lips. I will rejoice and be glad. May I create a radiant atmosphere of thanksgiving, Jesus, and may my joy overflow.

"Joy in the Lord has for its ground, knowledge of the Lord. In order to rejoice in the Lord, you must know the Lord not as you know a mere fact, but as you know a dear friend, a loving father, One who is the source of your life, the fountain of your good, the hope of your soul, the desire of your heart. Men are always tempted to rejoice, not in Him, but in themselves and the world; in their strength, their comforts, their advantages. But He shakes our security in these things, that we may live nearer to Him; that we may learn when and where only is the joy that remains; not written in the sand and washed out by every tide, but graven on the everlasting rock; and that by personal experience we may each one rejoice in Him alone – whatever betide – in Him for ever and ever." – H. Alford

A Strong Resolve

But as for me, I am like a green olive tree in the house of God; I trust [confidently] in the lovingkindness of God forever and ever. I will thank You forever, because You have done it, [You have rescued me and kept me safe]. I will wait on Your name, for it is good, in the presence of Your godly ones.

– Psalm 52:8-9 AMP

Through the wisdom of God, Solomon concluded that happiness and true satisfaction only come through our relationship with the Lord. Despite trials and persecution, Paul was continually happy because he was habitually thankful. Here in Psalm 52:8, David declared that he would flourish and thrive even though his enemies were seeking to destroy him. Wisdom, a grateful heart, and a strong resolve raise us above our circumstances and trials.

David was an exile running from King Saul when he wrote Psalm fifty-two. Saul had already attempted to kill him sixteen times. One day, David and his men were hungry. They stopped to seek assistance at the tabernacle in Nob. David asked Ahimilech the priest to provide him with food and weapons. He did not, however, tell him that they were running from Saul. The priest gave them some of the consecrated bread from the table of showbread as well as Goliath's sword, and then they went on their way. Unfortunately, Doeg, one of Saul's most loyal servants, happened to be there at the same time and overheard the entire exchange. David moved on to the land of the Philistines and then to the caves of Adulam. Doeg went back to Saul. Soon afterward, Saul, who was in a crazed mental state, began accusing all his guards of conspiring against him by protecting David because no one would tell him where David was hiding (1 Samuel 22:8). Doeg, full of ambition and evil motives, spoke up. He not only disclosed David's whereabouts, but he told Saul that Ahimilech the priest had helped David, even given him weapons. Saul was enraged. He summoned the priests of Nob to come before him and questioned them. Ahimilech admitted he had, indeed, helped David but maintained he had had no knowledge that there was any conflict between the two of them. Saul was completely irrational and ordered his men to kill all of the priests, all eighty-five of them. Saul's men, however, would not do it out of fear of the Lord.

Doeg was an ambitious man who sought after status and power. He saw his opportunity to gain favor with King Saul. You see, King Saul promised those he recruited positions in his government if they would help him catch and destroy David. Doeg rose to the occasion. Doeg, the Edomite, is first mentioned in First Samuel chapter twenty-one and verse seven. He is described as a servant of King Saul, Saul's chief shepherd, overseeing all the servants tending Saul's livestock. And apparently, he had a long-standing, antagonistic relationship with David. In Rabbinic literature, it is said that Doeg was the one who praised David in front of Saul in First Samuel, purposely provoking King Saul's jealousy toward David. He deliberately ascribed to David the very qualities that Saul was most obviously lacking, triggering his actions against David. That's just the way Doeg was. There had been some bad history between the two: David and Doeg. Ancient Jewish Rabbinic writings also indicate that David and Doeg had a sharp disagreement over determining where the site for the temple would be located.

Doeg seemed to be envious of David right from the very beginning and did everything that he could to tear David down. He tried to disprove David's lineage when the prophet Samuel was extending favor to David. In the Midrash, it is said that Doeg even tried to persuade King Saul to reject David's marriage to his daughter Michal. He encouraged Saul to give her to another man in marriage. The bottom line is that Doeg had been playing a big part in the conflict between Saul and David. He had been causing trouble for David for a very long time, and here in Psalm fifty-two, he betrays David once again. He saw an opportunity, and he seized it! Driven by a grudge and a desire to be promoted and lifted up, he stepped up. He stepped up and did Saul's dirty work. When the others refused to execute the priests of Nob, Doeg said that he would do it. He would obey the king's order. Doeg not only killed all of the priests, but he went way beyond Saul's command and also slaughtered the entire city of Nob—men, women, and children alike (1 Samuel 22:18-19). Doeg was a ruthless, conniving, and wicked man. He had no regard for David. He had no regard for the innocent people of Nob. And he had no regard for God.

Have you ever had someone in your life that had it in for you, even tried to make trouble for you? Have you ever had someone in your life tell lies about you, plant negative seeds in other people's minds about you, and betray you?

After the incident in Nob, David writes Psalm fifty-two.

> *Why do you boast in evil, O mighty man? The lovingkindness of God endures all day long. Your tongue devises destruction, like a sharp razor, working deceitfully. You love evil more than good, and falsehood more than speaking what is right. You love all words that devour, O deceitful tongue. But God will break you down forever; He will take you away and tear you away from your tent, and uproot you from the land of the living. The righteous will see it and fear, and will [scoffingly] laugh, saying, "Look [this is] the man who would not make God his strength [his stronghold and fortress], but trusted in the abundance of his riches, taking refuge in his wealth."*
> *– Psalm 52:1-7 AMP*

> *But as for me, I am like a green olive tree in the house of God; I trust [confidently] in the lovingkindness of God forever and ever. I*

will thank You forever, because You have done it, [You have rescued me and kept me safe.] I will wait on Your name, for it is good, in the presence of Your godly ones. – Psalm 52:8-9 AMP

Doeg was a man after his own self-promotion, position, and power. He did not follow God, God's principles, or place his trust in the Lord. He trusted in his own success and his own riches. He would have done anything to get ahead, including that which would destroy others in the process. David is making a declaration in this passage. He is declaring that the enemy will come to ruin. He is not cursing or speaking evil over his enemy. That's not what is happening here. This is not vindictive speech. It is more of a declaration of God being a just God who exercises judgment upon evil. And that is, in fact, what happened to Doeg. He did not repent, and his life came to ruin. It is thought that Doeg may have died a leper. Some believe that he was slain by his own pupils. Others maintain that David killed him when Doeg informed him of the death of Saul and of Jonathan. At any rate, such is the demise of the wicked. Sometimes it may seem as though the wicked are prospering and doing well. Do not be deceived. Whatever you sow you will also reap.

David, on the other hand, was a man after God's own heart. David trusted in God. He declared that he would be like a green olive tree: planted, rooted, growing, flourishing, and thriving even in the face of trouble. John Gill says that Psalm fifty-two and verse eight "expresses David's faith and confidence [that], notwithstanding his present troubles, he should be restored again, and be in a very flourishing condition."

What declaration will you make in the midst of trials and troubles? What declaration will you make in the face of fear and destruction?

But as for me, I am like a green olive tree in the house of God; I trust [confidently] in the lovingkindness of God forever and ever. – Psalm 52:8 AMP

PRAYER

Though evil seems to prevail all around me, I will trust confidently in You! In the midst of trouble and chaos, I can lay down and rest in peace. You, oh Lord, are a shield around me. You're my glory and the lifter of my head. When the enemy seems to be prevailing against me, my eyes will remain fixed on You. You rescue me and keep me safe. You are a strong, fortified tower, mighty fortress, and refuge in times of trouble. You surround me with songs of deliverance. The Angel of the Lord encamps around me. No weapon formed against me will prosper. Every tongue that rises against me in judgment, You will condemn. You vindicate me, Lord. This glorious triumph over opposition is the heritage of the servants of the Lord. And that I am. I am a servant of the most high God. You prepare a table before me in the presence of my enemies. Even there, You bless me. Even there, You cause me to flourish and prosper. I am like a green olive tree thriving in Your presence forever and ever. Amen.

I will thank You forever, because You have done it, [You have rescued me and kept me safe]. – Psalm 52:9a AMP

Anointed in His Presence

But I am like a flourishing olive tree, anointed in the house of God.
— Psalm 52:8a TPT

When evil seemed to prevail all around him, David held fast to his faith. Even in the midst of betrayal and danger, David trusted in the Lord. He had made up his mind that whatever trouble presented itself in his life, he would be like a flourishing olive tree. We may not know a whole lot about olive trees, but in Bible times, this was in fact a bold resolve. David was saying a lot when he made this declaration!

Olive trees are strong and durable. They grow on the bare, rocky ground, hills, and mountains. It's the rough terrain and the barren places in which they manage to thrive. They are able to adapt to their dry, hot climate where long summers are filled with heat and very little rainfall. They grow and flourish in this kind of environment anyway. Olive trees are known for their fruitfulness and longevity. They can live for thousands of years. There is actually an olive tree in Croatia dated 1,600 years old. It is still producing fruit today! Olive trees are most resilient, able to bounce back from frost, disease, and even fire. Remarkably, there are recorded instances of olive trees that appeared to be completely destroyed by these elements, yet new shoots appeared the following spring season. Deadwood was removed, and they began to produce fruit again. That is because the root system of an olive tree is capable of regenerating itself even when the above-ground structure of the tree is destroyed. Even if an olive tree is severely neglected, the tree will soon send up shoots from the roots all around the parent stem. And if a parent stem decays, these shoots are capable of taking its place.

Strong, durable, hardy, resilient, and fruitful, an olive tree can live for thousands of years and bear much fruit. Large olive trees can produce an average of four hundred plus pounds of olives annually. Older trees can produce even more. And we know that the fruit they produce has many health benefits. Olives and olive oil are full of antioxidants, healthy fats, and fiber. They are good for our overall health.

In Bible times, oil was used extensively in food and in medicine, burned in oil lamps for light, and poured out for the anointing of a person. Obtaining and processing the olive oil was quite a process. The olive trees were literally beaten and shaken until the olives fell to the ground and were gathered. Workers climbed the higher branches to retrieve the rest of the olives. The olives were then soaked in water to clean them and purge them of their bitterness. The bitter quality of the olive was removed in the soaking process. Next, the olives were crushed in the oil press to extract their oil. Sometimes they were trodden out by the feet. Today, the olives are crushed by heavy weights in oil mills. Usually, the berries are crushed, stones and all.

Shaking, beating, pressing, crushing—this was the process of getting the oil to flow. How many times have we felt like we have been shaken, beaten, pressed, and crushed by troubles in our lives? In verse two, David said, "I will thank You forever, because You have done it, [You have rescued me and kept me safe]." David had experienced God's faithfulness over and over again, and he had not forgotten. In Psalm 34:19, David confessed, "Many hardships and perplexing circumstances confront the righteous, but the Lord rescues him from them all." The Lord rescued David, and He will rescue us.

David had become strong and resilient. He had been through the process. He was determined that he would not only survive but also grow, flourish, thrive, and produce good fruit no matter what came against him.

But as for me, I am like a green olive tree in the house of God.
– Psalm 52:8a AMP

Where was it that David flourished and thrived? It was in the house of God, His dwelling place. The house of God in Psalm 52:8 translates as "in communion with Him" in the original Hebrew language. It is the place of His presence. That's the place that God is always calling us back to. It's the place of sweet intimacy with Him. And it is where we find assurance and a strong resolve in the midst of troubles.

David confidently trusted in God because he continually returned to the place of God's presence. He enjoyed fellowship and communion with the Lord, and the anointing of the Lord was upon him. The Passion Translation puts it like this:

*But I am like a flourishing olive tree, **anointed** in the house of God. – Psalm 52:8a TPT (Emphasis added)*

In God's presence, David received a fresh anointing of the strength and power of God to face anything. It was the place where he was cleansed and purged from any bitterness that may have wanted to attach itself to his heart. In God's presence, David was continually refreshed and renewed. David was able to praise the Lord and give Him thanks because he had spent time in His presence.

I trust in the unending love of God; his passion toward me is forever and ever. Because it is finished, I will praise you forever and give you thanks. Before all your godly lovers I will proclaim your beautiful name! – Psalm 52:8b-9TPT

Won't you place your confident trust in Him, even in the midst of your most challenging moments in life? Run to the place of His presence. Draw near to Him. Maintain sweet fellowship with the Lord. Become one of His godly lovers who proclaim His beautiful name, for He is good and His mercy endures forever. Remember His faithfulness. Praise

Him. Give thanks. Go ahead and triumph and rejoice and declare your victory in Jesus's mighty name.

 **PRAYER**

Lord, I have been through the process, and You have made me strong, durable, resilient, and able to bounce back! I have not forgotten Your faithfulness to me. It is because of Your faithfulness that I can stand and make bold and confident declarations. I have a strong resolve within me. I hold fast to my faith. Nothing can quench nor put out the fire of my passion for You, not troubles, not trials, not chaos. I refuse to become bitter. I am determined to become better. I have been shaken, beaten, pressed, and crushed by circumstances and situations, and my oil flows. It flows because You have anointed me. You have anointed me for Your purposes and for Your glory. You have anointed me with fresh strength and with power. You have anointed me in Your presence. Oh, how I love Your presence. It is because of Your presence that I experience steady and continued growth. It's because of Your presence that I am able to thrive in every season of my life. In Your presence is fullness of joy! That joy is mine.

I love You [fervently and devotedly], O Lord, my strength. – Psalm 18:1 AMP

Arise

Arise, my dearest. Hurry, my darling. Come away with me! I have come as you have asked to draw you to my heart and lead you out. For now is the time, my beautiful one. The season has changed, the bondage of your barren winter has ended, and the season of hiding is over and gone. The rains have soaked the earth and left it bright with blossoming flowers. The season for singing and pruning the vines has arrived. I hear the cooing of doves in our land, filling the air with songs to awaken you and guide you forth. Can you not discern this new day of destiny breaking forth around you? The early signs of my purposes and plans are bursting forth. The budding vines of new life are now blooming everywhere. The fragrance of their flowers whispers, "There is change in the air. Arise, my love, my beautiful companion, and run with me to the higher place. For now is the time to arise and come away with me."

– Song of Solomon 2:10-13 TPT

He is calling us to come away with Him to the place of His Presence. Now is the time! Remember, there is a time for everything: an opportune time, an appointed time, and a *right now* time. We must understand that there is a time to get up out of that stuck place and that hurt place and move forward to the healed place, the strengthened place, and the refreshed place. It is time to move to the place where our garden is growing and we are allowing our Gardener, God, to landscape our lives with His Word, till our hearts, and even remove some roots and weeds. It's time to flourish and thrive. It's time to sing, rejoice, and give thanks! And if the season for pruning has arrived, then so be it.

There is a process. That process is described in Scripture as grafting, growth, pruning, more growth, and the bearing of fruit. In Psalms chapter fifty-two and verse eight, David said that he was like an olive tree. When the Bible speaks of the process of grafting, it specifically uses the analogy of the grafting of olive trees. In Chapter eleven of Romans, Paul talks about Israel and its rejection of Christ. He refers to Israel, the Jews, as God's natural branches. He goes on to say that because of their unbelief, they were broken off. Then he says in verse seventeen that we (the Gentiles) were like wild olive trees. We were grafted in among them and became partakers of the roots and fatness of the olive tree. Paul warns us not to be arrogant or haughty but to fear God because if He did not spare His natural branches, He may not spare us either. He then tells us to remember that we do not support the root, but the root supports us. Paul continues to make the point that if the unbelieving Jews do not continue in their unbelief, they will be grafted in again. He says, "For if God grafted you in, even though you were taken from what is by nature a wild olive tree, how much more can he reconnect the natural branches by inserting them back into their own cultivated olive tree" (Romans 11:24)! In God's plan, Israel's rejection is temporary.

Relating to us, the Gentiles, we are like wild olive branches that have been grafted onto a domestic tree. Once grafted, we are then able to benefit from all the richness and the goodness of that tree. The people Paul was addressing in the book of Romans during this time would have understood this perfectly. They were very familiar with this process of grafting. What *does* this process of grafting look like?

Grafting

The wild olive trees are cut back. Slits are made on the freshly sawed branch ends, and a few grafts from a cultivated tree are inserted in a way that the bark of the small shoot of the branch aligns. The exposed ends are smeared with mud made from clay and then bound with cloth or date straw. This is held together by throngs made from the bark of young mulberry branches. This small shoot of a tree is inserted into another tree. The trunk (main stem) will support and nourish it. The two unite and become one tree. The fruit that is produced from it is good fruit. A wild olive branch grafted will thrive.

This is the beginning of our own process when it comes to our salvation, isn't it? We are grafted in. We are being cultivated and tended to by God. He sustains us. He nourishes us. We grow. We flourish. We bear fruit. And we rejoice. Then there is a time for pruning. John chapter fifteen and verse two says, "Every branch that bears fruit he prunes, that it may bear more fruit." Pruning is necessary.

In my state of South Carolina, peaches are considered our official state fruit. South Carolina produces an average of 54,600 tons of peaches a year and is second only to the state of California in peach production. In the area where I live, it is common to drive by peach orchards. Gorgeous pink blossoms paint the fields in the spring season. It is really something to behold against the Carolina blue skies. Those orchards are beautiful! However, pruning takes place in mid-February before the sap starts running. These same orchards are nothing to look at once all the trees have been cut back. Every year those limbs are cut back right to the trunk of the tree. It's not pretty. In his book "The Fruit of Christ's Presence," Harry Lee Poe talks about how he grew up in South Carolina going to a local peach orchard to pick peaches. He describes the peach trees that he remembers as having strong trunks and healthy foliage and being loaded with big, juicy peaches. Poe also remembers seeing those orchards after the branches had been cut back to the trunk and thinking that the pruning of the trees was such a waste. He often wondered why anyone would even do that to those strong, beautiful trees. Why didn't they just let those limbs keep growing and growing? Later in life, he moved to Kentucky with his family and their neighbors had a peach tree. They were not in the habit of pruning the tree. They *did* let their tree take its own course. And what Poe observed was that the tree's trunk was thin and willowy. There was barely any foliage on it. The foliage that it did have was scraggly. The tree was bare, with very little fruit to boast of. And the little bit of fruit that it did produce was small, hard, golf-ball-sized fruit. That peach tree wasn't anything like the trees he grew up seeing in South Carolina with the sturdy trunks, lush foliage, and large, ripe, juicy peaches that he once enjoyed. Pruning is not a waste after all, Friends. There is a good purpose for the pruning!

In the life of a Christian, pruning is not pretty. It can be painful. Similarly, the process is most beneficial, and it is a reward for a fruitful life. It is the growing, fruitful life that is pruned. God prunes the life of everyone who abides in Christ and produces fruit. He removes whatever has been inhibiting our continued growth, and He does it because He loves us. He prunes us so that we do not remain in that thin, willowy condition. Our Gardener, God, prunes us so that we can begin to thrive once again and in an even greater way!

In the pruning process of a tree, dead, rotting limbs are cut away. These limbs can quickly become diseased and even ridden with insects. And that situation can end up killing the entire tree. Dead things prevent fruitfulness. It is true in the life of a tree, and it's true in the life of a believer. It's good for us to regularly evaluate our own lives and ask ourselves, "Are there any dead things in my life that I need to leave behind? Have I been dragging around dead limbs that have not only weighed me down but also hindered my life from being as fruitful as it could be?" Ask the Lord right now if this is the case in your own life.

The Lord began to speak to me personally as I went through a recent transition from leaving behind a home that we had been living in for seven years and moving into a new home. The transition should have been filled with nothing but joy and excitement, but my beloved dog passed away the very day that we were making our move. My heart was absolutely broken. That dog had entered my life on the very first day I moved into the previous home and died on my final day there. She was an outdoor dog, somewhat wild and free. We were living on a property filled with woods and a creek. She was used to having her full roam of the woodsy environment. She had never been chained or leashed. There was no need for that. For three years we looked and looked for a home with a similar setting just for the dog! I was quite attached to her, and I was determined to take her with me no matter what. I felt confident that the new home we had now chosen would meet her needs, as she was getting up there in years. As the weeks drew closer to our moving day, I practiced getting her in and out of my car and accustomed to riding to prepare her for that big day. I had plans for that dog! She had been a part of my everyday life for seven years. Through tears that lasted weeks and even months, I asked the Lord to speak to me about the timing of her death. It clearly felt as if one season had ended in my life and a new season had begun in every way, including my time with this beautiful, loyal, humorous, entertaining, and loving dog. My husband called our oldest son and asked him to pray for me that tear-filled day. My son's response was that the timing of her passing was "beautiful." I wondered what he meant by that and inquired of the Lord.

I asked the Lord why He did not allow me to take my dog, that had brought me so much joy, into this new season with me. As hard as it was to hear, I felt the Lord saying to me that there are some things in our lives that have served us well in our previous season, but they cannot enter into our new season with us. They served us well in the last season, but they will not serve us well in the new season. I began to realize that every time we have made a transition from one season of our ministry life to another, we had to let go of something that was important to us. And it was painful. Those things may have been good things, even things that brought us much joy in that last season. However, they would not be a part of the new season. I thought about how many times I had tried to hold on to something from a previous season as I transitioned into the next. Had holding on, looking back, and grieving their loss kept me from fully embracing the new or from being as fruitful as I could have been? Even though the things that were being severed may have been fruitful in the previous season, they were now over, done, expired. And we cannot drag the dead things into the new season. As morbid as that may sound in relation to a beloved pet, the truth that the Lord was speaking to my heart wasn't about my cherished pet at all. He was showing me a picture of dragging the dead limbs from the previous season into a new season. The things that I had become attached to and grown fond of—even the things that I had become dependent upon, drew strength from, found comfort in, and experienced joy with—these things are often severed in order to receive more. They have served their purpose. Their time has expired. Some things in our lives are truly seasonal. We must learn to discern the seasons and allow God to have His way. Hold on to nothing so tightly that you cannot release it in order to arise and move to higher places with the Lord.

There is change in the air. Arise, my love, my beautiful companion, and run with me to the higher place. For now is the time to arise and come away with me. – Song of Solomon 2:13 TPT

 **PRAYER**

Help me, Lord, to discern the shifting of the seasons that I might transition from one to the next well. You have new things for me! It's a new day. It's a new season. Help me to willingly release anything that I must release in order to receive Your best. Thank You, for the blessings of the last season. I am now ready to arise and run with You to higher places! May a new day of destiny truly break forth around me in Jesus's name.

The season for singing and pruning the vines has arrived. I hear the cooing of doves in our land, filling the air with songs to awaken you and guide you forth. – Song of Solomon 2:11 TPT

Vital Union with Christ

I am the true vine, and my Father is the gardener.
– John 15:1 NIV

Jesus said that He is the true vine and that His Father, God, is the gardener. Other Bible versions may use the word farmer, husbandman, or vinedresser. What does a gardener or a vinedresser do? He is the keeper of the vineyard—tending, guarding, defending, and protecting it. He is the cultivator. He engrafts the branches into the vine. He is concerned about the growth and the welfare of his tree, so he tends the vine and cares for the branches. He is interested in its strength and health, so he cuts off the unfruitful and useless branches. And He prunes the fruitful branches so they will become even stronger, healthier, and MORE fruitful.

> *I am the true Vine, and My Father is the vinedresser. Every branch in Me that does not bear fruit, He takes away; and every branch that continues to bear fruit, He [repeatedly] prunes, so that it will bear more fruit [even richer and finer fruit]. – John 15:1-2 AMP*

Pruning is the work of the gardener. The dead, useless limbs and branches are cut off and taken away, but the branches that have been fruitful are shown great care and are trimmed. They are pruned again and again. It is important for the believer in Christ to know that pruning is not a form of punishment but, rather, a reward for a fruitful life. It is an act of love and great care. It is evidence of a life that is producing fruit. In the life of every growing believer, there is a time for pruning.

"The pruning or cleansing is not the removal of weeds or thorns or anything from the outside that may hinder the growth. No. It's the cutting off of the long shoots of the previous year, the removal of something that comes from within, that has been produced by the life of the vine itself. It is the removal of something that is a proof of the vigor of its life. The more vigorous the growth season has been, the greater the need for the pruning. It is the honest, healthy wood of the vine that has to be cut away. And why? Because it would consume too much of the sap to fill all the long shoots of last year's growth: the sap must be saved up and used for fruit alone." – Andrew Murray

This life-giving, nourishing, and sustaining sap comes from the vine. In John chapter fifteen and verse one, Jesus says that He is the *true* Vine. All that we need for growth, vitality, and a fruitful life comes from Him. He is our source, and He provides all we need. The natural vines of the earth are a picture of Jesus and an expression of who He is.

I am the Vine; you are the branches. The one who remains in Me and I in him bears much fruit, for [otherwise] apart from Me [that is, cut off from vital union with Me] you can do nothing. If anyone does not remain in Me, he is thrown out like a [broken off] branch, and withers and dies. – John 15:5-6a AMP

Once again, in verse five, Jesus says that He is the Vine. He goes on to say that we are the branches. Our growth and fruitfulness come only through our union with Christ. Remaining connected to the Vine is vital. We cannot flourish and produce fruit without His life-giving, life-producing supply.

I have never seen this metaphor demonstrated more clearly than the day we moved into our present home. It was one hundred degrees that day. If you have ever moved, especially after thirty-two years of marriage and the raising of three kids, then you know how much stuff you have acquired and how much work is involved. Between the South Carolina summertime heat and the discovery of my beloved pet's passing, my physical, mental, and emotional energy had been sucked right out of me. Still, we hustled from sunup till sundown. Lining the driveway of our new home were Crepe Myrtle trees in full bloom, some dark burgundy in color and others a soft purple. As my exhausted husband pulled into the driveway with the moving truck, he didn't realize how tall that truck was. And the top of the truck struck many of the low-hanging branches of those beautiful trees, breaking several completely off. We were not happy about it, but we had to keep moving. We needed to keep on task, so we dragged those flowering branches off to the side, behind the fence, and out of sight. Several weeks later, there they were. While the branches that remained on the trees were still full and flourishing, these limbs were now bare except for a few dry, brown, crunchy leaves. There was no longer any evidence of the bright, colorful, vibrant flowers that once decorated their limbs. In fact, the limbs themselves looked as if they had shrunk. They appeared smaller. The broken-off branches were dry, brittle, and shriveled. They were withering more and more with each passing day. The branches were barely recognizable. As we dragged them away, the dry pieces literally snapped and broke away. In such a short time, these once healthy branches had become nothing but deadwood. There was no life left in them separated from their source. It had rained a handful of times during the weeks those branches laid upon the ground behind that fence. Nevertheless, any water source from an outside force did not revive the branches. Without that life-giving, life-producing connectedness to their source, they would never produce anything again. What a vivid picture of John chapter fifteen.

When you're joined with me and I with you, the relation intimate and organic, the harvest is sure to be abundant. Separated, you can't produce a thing. Anyone who separates from me is deadwood. –
John 15:5b-6a MSG

A vinedresser has a purpose. A vine has a purpose. And a branch also has a purpose. The purpose of a branch is to produce fruit. God's plan is to make you a fruitful branch. In his book *The True Vine*, Andrew Murray makes this very powerful and thought-provoking statement:

> "The object of my being a branch, the one mark of my being a true branch, the one condition of my abiding and growing strong, is that I bear fruit of the heavenly Vine for dying men to eat and live."

Murray says that we become branches, "through whom the Spirit flows and brings God's life to men!" More fruit is produced by "allowing His glory to shine out through us, by yielding ourselves to Him, that His glory may manifest itself in us and through us to the world."

And there it is. It is in the abiding, the maintaining of that vital union with Christ, that we bear such fruit. It's in the yielded and connected life that we become fruitful and useful for the kingdom of God. Apart from Him, we can do nothing. We cannot bear fruit by our own gifts and talents alone. We cannot produce fruit by our own efforts, by working harder, or by trying harder. We cannot produce His fruit by our own striving and straining. This fruitful life is dependent upon one thing and one thing only. The flourishing, thriving, fruitful life is directly tied to remaining connected to Jesus, the Vine.

In verse sixteen, Jesus said, "I have planted you that you might go and bear fruit" (AMP). It is God's purpose for us to be healthy, fruit-bearing believers. The fruitful life of the believer brings honor and glory to God.

My Father is glorified and honored by this, when you bear much fruit, and prove yourselves to be My (true) disciples. – John 15:8 AMP

Have you been maintaining your vital union with the Lord, or have you felt somewhat disconnected? Have you been bearing all the fruit that Jesus, the true Vine, is wanting to produce through you?

If you live in Me [abide vitally united to Me] and My words remain in you and continue to live in your hearts, ask whatever you will, and it shall be done for you. – John 15:7 AMPC

 **PRAYER**

Thank You, Jesus, for Your great care and love that You demonstrate toward me. I consent to the pruning and cleansing process. Remove the dead, useless things from my life. You are my source. You provide all that I need. Thank You for Your life-giving and sustaining supply! Nourish me and make me a fruitful branch. Let Your Spirit flow through me unhindered. Let it be a strong flow that literally brings life to others, especially those who have been living without You, Jesus. May I be a healthy fruit-bearing believer, useful for the Kingdom of God. May my life bring honor and glory to Your Name. I am putting an end to all striving and straining today and giving my full focus, time, and energy to maintaining my vital union and connectedness with You, Father. You are the true Vine. I am Your branch.

"The branch has but one object for which it exists, one purpose to which it is entirely given up, to bear the fruit the vine wishes to bring forth. And so the believer has but one reason for being a branch – but one reason for his existence on earth – that the heavenly vine may through him bring forth His fruit. Happy is the soul that knows this, that has consented to it, and that says, 'I've been redeemed and live for one thing.'" – Andrew Murray

Eat and Drink

*Remain in Me, and I [will remain] in you. Just as no branch can bear
fruit by itself without remaining in the vine, neither can you [bear fruit,
producing evidence of your faith] unless you remain in Me. I am the Vine;
you are the branches. The one who remains in Me and I in him bears
much fruit, for [otherwise] apart from Me [that is, cut off from vital
union with Me] you can do nothing. If anyone does not remain in Me, he
is thrown out like a [broken off] branch, and withers and dies; and they
gather such branches and throw them into the fire, and they are burned. If
you remain in Me and My words remain in you [that is, if we are vitally
united and My message lives in your heart], ask whatever you wish and it
will be done for you. My Father is glorified and honored by this, when you
bear much fruit, and prove yourselves to be My [true] disciples.*

– John 15:4-8 AMP

We are branches that have been grafted in. We enjoy the richness and
the goodness of the Vine. We are connected in intimate fellowship and
continued communion. Watered, fed, nourished, fertilized, and pruned,
we continue to grow, flourish, thrive, and produce fruit. We are pruned
season after season in order to produce even more fruit, fruit that lasts.
This fruit brings honor to God and glorifies Him. We always remain
attached to our source. We understand that everything hinges on this
abiding. To abide means to stay and *not* to depart. It means to remain
as one and to live or dwell together.

Sustenance

In John chapter six verses thirty-one through thirty-three, Jesus said that Moses gave the Israelites bread (manna) in the desert to sustain them, but His Father gives the true bread from Heaven to the world. In verse thirty-five, Jesus goes on to say that He, Himself, is the Bread of Life.

"I am the Bread of Life." – John 6:35a NKJV

Jesus refers to Himself as the true bread sent into the world by God to sustain the soul and spiritual life of man. This word "life" in verse thirty-five is the word *zoe* in the original Hebrew language, and it translates as "the absolute fullness of life, both essential and ethical, which belongs to God." It refers to "life real and genuine, a life active and vigorous, devoted to God, blessed in the portion even in this world."

"I am the living bread which came down from heaven. If anyone eats of this bread, he will live forever; and the bread that I shall give is My flesh, which I shall give for the life of the world." – John 6:51 NKJV

Again in verse fifty-one, Jesus says, "I am the Living Bread." In this verse, the word used for "living" in the original Greek language is the word *zao*. This word is a little different from the word *zoe*. It translates as "having vital power in itself and exerting the same power upon the soul." The word *zao* also means "to live, to breathe, to enjoy real life, and to have true life, life worthy of the name blessed." Metaphorically, it means to be full of vigor, to be fresh, strong, and efficient. Jesus said to come to Him every day and partake of this bread that gives *zao* (life). The bread that He offered was Himself. Jesus is the true bread, and He is the true drink.

Living Water

As the woman at the well came to fill her water pot in John chapter four, Jesus spoke to her about "living" water. This was a woman who spent her whole life searching for something to fill her own personal emptiness, to satisfy the void within, and to find love and happiness. Jesus said to this woman:

> *"Whoever drinks of the water that I shall give him will never thirst. But the water that I shall give him will become in him a fountain of water springing up into everlasting life." – John 4:14 NKJV*

This water that Jesus offered was Himself. Later, in John chapter thirty-seven, verses thirty-seven through thirty-nine, Jesus speaks of the "living" water again:

> *"If anyone thirsts, let him come to Me and drink. He who believes in Me, as the Scripture has said, out of his heart will flow rivers of living water." But this He spoke concerning the Spirit, whom those believing in Him would receive; for the Holy Spirit was not yet given, because Jesus was not yet glorified. – John 7:37b-39 NKJV*

In verse thirty-seven, the word "anyone" applies to you, and it applies to me. This invitation to come and drink is for us, today. Jesus told the woman at the well that anyone who drinks this water will never thirst again. Nothing else has the means to quench our thirst and bring true life with it like Jesus. If we try to fill ourselves with anything other than Christ, our thirst may be quenched for a little while, but it will not last. Soon, we will be thirsting again, and we will be looking for something else to fill us. And something else, and something else. The woman at the well sought happiness and found only misery and disappointment. Her inner water pot leaked. When Jesus found the woman at the well that day, she had come to the well with an empty water pot, an empty heart, and an empty spirit. And He offered her living water. Matthew Henry says, "The living waters he would give would yield a lasting satisfaction and bliss."

This Living Water never fails! It is an ever-present, ever-ready well that quenches us. It also flows to others and springs up into eternal life. It continually revives the soul and gives life!

Life

Human life can only survive for between one or two months without food. The body needs the nutrients in food to survive. It uses protein, carbohydrates, fats, vitamins, and minerals to renew cells and fuel bodily processes. Without food, the body will begin to break down its own tissue for consumption, even muscle tissue including the heart. The body's organs will begin to shut down. All body systems will be affected, including the brain. While we might be able to survive for weeks without food, we can only survive a few days without water. Our bodies need a continual supply of water. Water repairs and maintains cells. Water is needed for almost every process in the human body. Without water, the body is unable to function properly and will begin to stop working. Hydration is vital for survival.

Like the bread and the water that sustains the human body, Jesus, the Bread of Life and the Living Water, sustains our spiritual life. He is our source! He is the true Bread, the true Water, and the true Vine. And the true Vine provides the branches with all the nutrients it needs to not only survive but to also thrive and to bear fruit that lasts. Today, He says to us, "Come eat. Come drink." Jesus extended this invitation to His disciples, and they responded, "Give us this bread." Jesus extended this invitation to the woman at the well, and she responded, "Give me this living water." Today, the offer still stands. How will you respond?

And the Spirit and the bride say, "Come!" And let him who hears say, "Come!" And let him who thirsts come. Whoever desires, let him take the water of life freely. – Revelations 22:17 NKJV

PRAYER

Lord, I come. I eat and I drink deeply. I partake of the Bread of Life and the Living Water every single day, for You sustain me. My life is a life devoted to God. Fill me with the fulness of life—real, genuine life, life worthy of the name blessed. Give me the quality of life that is filled with satisfaction and bliss that is only found in You.

"I am the Bread of Life. Come every day to me and you will never be hungry. Believe in me and you will never be thirsty." – John 6:35 TPT

An Invited Guest

You have not chosen Me, but I have chosen you and I have appointed and placed and purposefully planted you, so that you would go and bear fruit and keep on bearing, and that your fruit will remain and be lasting, so that whatever you ask of the Father in My name [as My representative] He may give you.

– John 15:16 AMP

Jesus is the Vine, and we are the branches. We have been chosen, appointed, placed, and purposefully planted. The King James Version of John 15:16 uses the words chosen and ordained. The Passion translation uses the words chosen and commissioned. And in the Aramaic, this word "chosen" translates like this: "I have invited you (as dinner guests)."

Yes, Lord, we accept your invitation, and we have come to your table!

Because we have been invited, chosen, appointed, ordained, and commissioned to bear fruit, God means to empower us, equip us, and answer our prayers. When we remain connected to our true source, we are in the right position. When we have made intimate communion with Him a habit and are full of His presence, full of His Word, and full of faith, we will find that our prayers are in harmony with the will of God. When our hearts are aligned with His heart, we will be praying Spirit-led prayers that get answers!

He is the Bread of Life, the Living Water, and the True Vine. Because of Jesus, the true Vine, we have access to an ever-present, ever-ready, life-giving spring that is always flowing. There is a life-producing fountain within us. He is the true and essential life of His people. And the life Jesus gives us is a fruitful and abundant life!

Life Abundant

The thief does not come except to steal, and to kill, and to destroy. I have come that they may have life and that they may have it more abundantly. – John 10:10b NKJV

Jesus said that He came to give us life and to give it to us more abundantly. What did He mean by that? The *Jamieson, Fausset, and Brown's Commentary on the Whole Bible* says that He came "not merely to preserve but impart life, and communicate it in rich and unfailing exuberance." This word "abundantly" is defined as "more even than they can possibly use." Wow! How much of this abundance have we been accessing?

The word "abundantly" in John 10:10 is the word *perissos* in the original Greek language, and it means "over and above, and more than is necessary." How can that be? Albert Barnes says that having life more abundantly means, "Literally, that they may have abundance, or that which abounds. The word denotes that which is not absolutely essential to life, but which is superadded to make life happy. They shall not merely have life—simple, bare existence—but they shall have all those superadded things which are needful to make that life eminently blessed and happy."

What has Jesus added to your life that you did not have before receiving Him as your Lord and Savior and before coming into a personal relationship with Him?

The term *perissos* life (abundant life) translates as "an uncommon life." It also translates as a more excellent or superior life. Having abundant life is having life to the fullest through the indwelling Spirit of God. When we receive Christ into our hearts, His Spirit dwells within us. J. Oswald Dykes puts it beautifully when he says that "Man's conversion to God adds a fresh region, a new department, to his being; it gives him new thoughts, it quickens in him new emotions, it begets new motives, it sets before him new ambitions. The new life must be a fuller one, a deeper one, than the old, giving birth to thoughts more grave, feelings more deep—in a word, 'life more abundant.'" Dykes goes on to say that the object or effect of our Christianity is not to deaden our interests of this life with its common joys and sorrows but to render our earthly life "larger and more intense."

Abundant Life: A Larger Life

"Our little life, obscure or petty as it may be, is no longer as a landlocked lake, set by itself apart; but, lo! It is an inlet, with open channel uniting it to the awful ocean beyond, and into it also there pour day after day those mysterious tides of life and passion which come from the infinite heart of the most high and loving One." – J. Oswald Dykes

Abundant life is an expanded life! It is a life that was meant to be enjoyed, and it is a life that is so full that it overflows.

I came that they may have and enjoy life, and have it in abundance [to the full, till it overflows.] – John 10:10b AMP

That's abundance! And we access this abundance through our vital union with Christ. The life that Jesus, the Vine, dispenses to us is a more excellent, expanded, full, uncommon life and a life of joy.

I have loved you just as the Father has loved Me; remain in My love [and do not doubt My love for you]. If you keep My commandments and obey My teaching, you will remain in My love, just as I have kept My Father's commandments and remain in His love. I have told

you these things so that My joy and delight may be in you, and that your joy may be made full and complete and overflowing. – John 15:9-11 AMP

His Joy in Us

Jesus was referring to the things concerning the vine and branches: His abiding in them and their abiding in Him, His love for them and their love for Him. Faithful and fruitful believers are His joy. And joy is what He also gives to us. It is a joy that is full and overflowing.

The word "joy" in John chapter fifteen and verse eleven is the word *chara* in the original Greek language, and it translates as "gladness, cheerfulness, calm delight, and to be exceedingly joyful!" Jesus came that we might have life abundantly, full of joy! The joy that He gives remains. The joy that comes from the world comes and goes, but the joy of those who abide in Christ is a lasting joy. Matthew Henry says, "The joy of the hypocrite is but for a moment, but the joy of those who abide in Christ's love is a continual feast." It's a feast. It's a smorgasbord! And you and I are invited dinner guests.

Jesus said that He purposed that our joy would remain and that it would be full! Adam Clarke says that this expression "that your joy may be full" is a metaphor taken from a vessel into which water or any other thing is poured until it is full to the brim.

Full to the Brim

How full is your vessel? Come to His table and partake of His continual feast until you are full and overflowing. And remember, you can keep coming back for more!

You're blessed when you've worked up a good appetite for God. He's food and drink in the best meal you'll ever eat. – Mt 5:6 MSG

PRAYER

Lord, I am Your holy vessel. Fill me with Your overflowing joy. Thank You for abundant life. More life and joy than I even need is at my disposal, and I haven't always known how to access it. Release to me all the superadded things that will make my life eminently blessed and happy as I abide in You. Oh, that I might walk in this uncommon life. Cause my life to become larger, more excellent, and more intense. Let it be a life that knows no boundaries. And let me experience a fuller, deeper joy than I've ever known before, in Jesus's name.

These things I have spoken to you, that My joy may remain in you, and that your joy may be full. – John 15:11 NKJV

Come Closer

*Because of you, I know the path of life, as I taste the
fulness of joy in your presence.*

— Psalm 16:11a TPT

God loves His children and delights in their joy and happiness. He
came to give us life abundantly. He imparts to us joy overflowing.
David, the Psalmist, had experienced this abundant life. David knew
this overflowing joy of the Lord. He knew it firsthand, and he found it
in God's presence. David said that he, himself, was like a green olive tree
in the presence of God. He also said that those of us who are planted in
God's presence flourish and bring forth fruit. Despite David's personal
failures, tragedies, and trials, he was able to experience a deep inner joy
because He remained near to the Lord. His jubilant heart was spilling
over when he expressed the following words to God.

*For just one day of intimacy with you is like a thousand days of joy
rolled into one. — Psalm 84:10a TPT*

Oh, to taste and experience and know this joy! You and I may desire
this kind of joy, but the truth is we *need* the joy of the Lord. Proverbs
17:22 says, "A joyful, cheerful heart brings healing to both the body
and soul. But the one whose heart is crushed struggles with sickness
and depression" (TPT).

Joy or Grief

In reference to this Scripture, John Gill says, "The joy or grief of the mind, those passions of the soul, have a great influence upon the body, either for its good or hurt." This is so true. We see it all around us, especially in the lives of those who are hurting. Many people we encounter day to day have experienced pain and grief so deep that they cannot seem to pull themselves out of a dark place. And so often, the grief within the soul begins to manifest or show up in one's physical body. It makes perfect sense. We are three-part beings, created with a spirit, soul, and body. And one part always affects the others. When we are struggling in our minds and emotions, it tends to show up in our physical bodies. Likewise, when we are sick in our physical bodies, it can wear on the mind and emotions. Medical studies indicate that many physical conditions are linked to mental issues, emotional trauma, and uncontrolled stress. Those studies confirm what God says in His Word, "The one whose heart is crushed struggles with sickness and depression." Adam Clarke says, "Nothing has such a direct tendency to ruin health and waste out life as grief, anxiety, fretfulness, bad tempers, etc. All these work death." Joy, on the other hand, brings forth healing to both the body and soul! We need the joy of the Lord, Friend.

> "Cheerfulness of spirit has a great influence upon the body, and much contributes to the health and welfare of it; and especially a heart of spiritual joy, peace of conscience, flowing from the blood of Christ, joy in the Holy Ghost, a rejoicing in Christ Jesus and his righteousness, and in the hope of the glory of God, much affect the outward man." – John Gill

A heart filled with joy is a good medicine! And God desires to fill us with His joy. He desires for us to be healed and whole. This is why He continually calls to us and even beckons us to come to Him. To those who are weary and weighed down with many burdens, He says, "Come!"

*Come to Me, all you who labor and are heavy-laden and
overburdened, and I will cause you to rest [I will ease and relieve
and refresh your souls]. – Matthew 11:28 AMPC*

To those who are dry and thirsty, He says, "Come!" To those who are
feeling depleted and empty, He says, "Come!"

*Let him who is listening say, Come! And let everyone come who
is thirsty [who is painfully conscious of his need of those things
by which the soul is refreshed, supported, and strengthened]; and
whoever [earnestly] desires to do it, let him come, take, appropriate,
and drink the water of Life without cost. – Revelation 22:17 AMPC*

Do you hear Him calling today?

Come Closer

*Pay attention and come closer to me, and hear, that your total being
may flourish. – Isaiah 55:3a TPT*

The Holy Spirit of God is always calling us to come closer and draw
near to Him. Christ is our true source. In Him, we are filled, sustained,
and satisfied. We access this soul abundance in His presence. He
disperses His joy to us as we abide in Him. In the place of His presence,
we find refreshing, relief, restoration, and healing. As we receive
from the Lord, our total being—spirit, soul, and body—flourishes.
He is the Vine, and we are the branches. It is in the place of intimate
relationship with Jesus that we find all that we have need of. It's in the
connected life. A connected life is an abundant life. A connected life is
a healthy life. A connected life is a life of joy. And the joy of the Lord is
our strength!

The Amplified Bible puts Isaiah 55:3 like this: "Incline your ear [to
listen] and come to Me; Hear, so that your soul may live." The word
"soul" in this Scripture refers to the inner being, the activity of the

mind, emotions, and even the activity of the will. And this word "live" means to be restored to health. Jesus is the great restorer. He is the Lord God our healer. In what condition do you find yourself today: joy, grief, or somewhere in between? Are you struggling with sickness and depression? Does your mind need to be renewed? Come to Jesus and receive from Him. Does your heart need to be healed? Does your soul need to be refreshed? Draw near to the Lord. Does your spirit need to be lifted? Does your body need to be restored and strengthened? Allow Christ to fill you with His joy! The state of the heart, the state of the soul, and the state of one's mental and emotional health and overall well-being must be nurtured from within. This nurturing comes from Christ Jesus.

> "The source of spiritual life is within; it cannot be inaccessible; it does not depend on anything from which we may be separated. And this is man's victory and end when within himself he has the source of life and joy, so he is independent of circumstances, of position, of things present and things to come." – *The Expositor's Bible Commentary*

It's Christ in us, the hope of Glory! I don't know what has been subtracting from your peace, your joy, and your happiness, but I do know where you can find it once again. It's in the place of His presence. We have been invited to come close and be filled that our total being might absolutely flourish. He is calling us to come near to Him today. The word "come" in the previous scriptures translates as "to be continuously coming." Jesus continues to draw us to Himself by the urgings of His Spirit. We must continue to hearken to His voice and keep company with Him.

It's good for me to draw near to God. – Psalm 73:28a NKJV

PRAYER

Lord, I love Your presence. I want nothing else but to be near you. Today, I press in a little closer. I'm shutting out the constant activity in my life—all of the busyness, the noise, and the distractions—with a desire to sit in your presence and receive from You. Speak to my heart. Allow me to experience a spirit-to-Spirit encounter with the lover of my soul, the kind of encounter that changes everything. Bring the relief and refreshing that I need—spirit, soul, and body. As I keep company with You, release to me this joy, and let it become a healing agent within my total being. Here's my cup, Lord. Fill it up and make me whole.

So listen carefully to me and you'll enjoy a sumptuous feast delighting in the finest of food. Pay attention and come closer to me, and hear; that your total being may flourish. – Isaiah 55:2b-3a TPT

The Main Course

Fill your thoughts with my words until they penetrate deep into your spirit. Then as you unwrap my words, they will impart true life and radiant health into the very core of your being.

– Proverbs 4:21-22 TPT

We have been invited to draw near to God. We must live intimately joined to Him. When we abide in Him, we access full life and overflowing joy! He is our source, and we draw from His stores that never run dry. Everything we need is found in His presence. David loved God's presence, and there he found joy. He was not alone. Solomon came to this same conclusion. Paul learned the lesson well. Many men and women of the Bible knew this unceasing and sustaining flow of life and joy because they knew the importance of remaining near to the Lord. They understood that satisfaction, contentment, happiness, and joy all rest on the love of God and fellowship with Him. These saints of God were filled with great joy and great hope because of God's presence in their lives. It was a lasting joy and a lasting hope that could not be taken away from them or squelched by adversity.

> "The hope in which Paul and the other disciples had even in their future inheritance enabled them to rejoice and be glad in the midst of trials and persecution. It not only sustained them, but it made them happy. That must be a valuable religion which will make people happy in the midst of persecutions and heavy calamities." – *Albert Barnes' Notes on the Entire Bible*

This "religion" that Albert Barnes speaks of is a close, personal relationship with Jesus Christ. Abundant life and joy are not dependent on circumstances, position, or things past, present, or to come. Happiness must have an inward source. That inward source is Christ. Do outside factors impact us and affect us negatively at times? You bet they do. However, Jesus said, "Keep company with me and you'll learn to live freely and lightly" (Matthew 11:30 MSG).

Learn to Live Freely and Lightly

In Luke chapter ten, Mary wanted nothing else but to be near Jesus. She put everything else aside just to keep company with Him. As she sat at His feet, she found herself hanging on to every word He spoke. Mary was caught up in the fellowship and communion with the Lord.

> *As they continued their travel, Jesus entered a village. A woman by the name of Martha welcomed him and made him feel quite at home. She had a sister, Mary, who sat before the Master, hanging on every word he said.* – Luke 10:38-39 MSG

Mary's sister, Martha, loved Jesus dearly and welcomed Him into her home. She was eager to serve Jesus. She went right to work and began preparing a meal for Jesus and her other guests, but she was pulled away by all she had to do in the kitchen. Soon, she felt overwhelmed by the busyness of all the tasks at hand.

> *But Martha [overly occupied and too busy] was distracted with much serving; and she came up to Him and said, Lord, is it nothing to You that my sister has left me to serve alone? Tell her then to help me [to lend a hand and do her part along with me]!* – Luke 10:40 AMPC

Not only was Martha exasperated with all the chores, but she began to feel sorry for herself. She complained in her heart, and then she complained aloud. Martha even assumed that Jesus didn't care. Jesus recognized the condition of her heart and tenderly addressed it,

"Martha, Martha, you are worried and bothered and anxious about so many things" (Luke 10:41 AMP). Martha had gotten herself all worked up. Stress, being overwhelmed, and feelings of dissatisfaction and discontentment set in quickly. That is what happens when we become disconnected from our source. Martha was about to learn something that Mary had already discovered.

> "Martha, Martha, you are worried and bothered and anxious about so many things; but only one thing is necessary, for Mary has chosen the good part [that which is to her advantage], which will not be taken away from her." – Luke 10:41-42 AMP

> "Mary has discovered the one thing most important by choosing to sit at my feet. She is undistracted, and I won't take this privilege from her." – Luke 10:42 TPT

Jesus told Martha that this one thing is necessary. It's vital. It's needed! It was actually the very thing that Martha needed the most and the thing that would bring health and healing to her very soul. It was the one thing that would refresh and revive her total being. The truth is that Martha was doing so many things right. She genuinely loved Jesus. She welcomed Him and made him feel right at home. Then she began getting a meal ready. She wanted everything to be just perfect. It was important to her. However, she was rushing and stressing with the preparations themselves. Finally, Jesus let her know that she was missing the most important ingredient. She was running around trying to serve Him, but all her activity had virtually kept her from Him. Jesus said that this time spent with Him would in essence be the main course!

> One thing only is essential, and Mary has chosen it—it's the main course. – Luke 10:42a MSG

Martha focused all her attention on serving and lost sight of the importance of spending time with the *one* she was serving. How did she miss this one central thing? I'm afraid that many times we've missed this too. And today we must be reminded, lest we find ourselves in this same condition that Martha found herself in. Martha was troubled by many things, and if we are not careful, we can become distracted by the troubles and difficulties of life. And worse, we can begin to feel disconnected from Jesus, our source of life and joy! Even the children of God who love Jesus and are faithful in serving Him can find themselves disconnected from the very one whom they are serving! Let's make sure that even in our daily activity we do not lose sight of the one thing that is most important. In the striving to be productive and accomplish what we desire and even what we must, let us not forget to give first place to Jesus. He fills us and satisfies us in a way that nothing and no one else can.

The sweet fellowship with the Lord is the main course, Friend. He's food and drink in the best meal you'll ever eat! If we are going to disconnect from anything, let's disconnect from all the activity, noise, and chaos of our lives and come before the Lord. If we are going to allow ourselves to become overwhelmed with anything, let us become overwhelmed by the love that Christ has for us. Like Mary, let's sit at His feet and hold on to every Word that He is speaking. Let's get caught up in the fellowship and communion with our Jesus.

> *I sat down in his shade and his fruit was sweet to my taste. He brought me to his banqueting table and his banner over me was love.*
> *– Song of Solomon 2:3-4 NKJV*

PRAYER

Oh, to be caught up in fellowship with You, Jesus. I just want to sit at your feet and commune with You. It's my one desire, and it's my privilege. I cherish my time spent with You, and I make it my priority. As the deer pants for streams of water, so my soul pants for You. My soul longs for the Living God. There is no one like You, Jesus. You have captured my heart. Your love is intoxicating, and it never disappoints. The anointing of your presence satisfies me like nothing else. You are such a rich banquet of pleasure to my soul. You satisfy me more than the richest feast. You continually draw me to Yourself. And I continuously come before You. Give me an undistracted devotion for you, Lord. I will remain under the banner of Your love, and I will praise You with songs of joy!

Rise up, my love, my fair one and come away with me. – Song of Solomon 2:10 NKJV

CLOSING

From the Shadows to the Substance

Now arise in the fulness of your union with the Lord.
– Philippians 4:1b TPT

David loved God's presence, and despite hardships and trouble, he experienced joy. Paul was trained by his troubles and learned to be content in every circumstance. Paul had found the recipe for being happy. Mary discovered it, too. Martha found herself pulled away, distracted, disconnected, upset, and troubled by many things. Jesus gently pointed her to the one thing that would truly fill her and satisfy her soul. He said that Mary had "chosen" this one thing. Apparently, it was Mary's choice. It was what she chose to do. Martha could have chosen it, too. And you and I must choose as well.

> *"Behold, I stand at the door and knock. If anyone hears my voice and opens the door, I will come in to him and dine with him, and he with me." – Revelation 3:20 NKJV*

Although Revelation 3:20 is a scripture often used as an invitation to receive Jesus as Lord and Savior, it was originally spoken to the believers of the Laodicean church in Asia Minor who had become apathetic towards the things of the Lord. Laodicea was a very prosperous city. It was known for having a well-respected financial center, a thriving textile industry, and a leading medical school. The people of Laodicea boasted of not needing a thing. They had become arrogant and self-satisfied people. The name Laodicea itself means self-righteousness. And that they were. The Lord addressed this very attitude in the following verses of Revelation chapter three.

> *"I know all the things you do, that you are neither hot nor cold. I wish that you were one or the other! But since you are like lukewarm water, neither hot nor cold, I will spit you out of my mouth! You say, 'I am rich. I have everything I want. I don't need a thing!' And you don't realize that you are wretched and miserable and poor and blind and naked. So I advise you to buy gold from me—gold that has been purified by fire. Then you will be rich. Also buy white garments from me so you will not be shamed by your nakedness, and ointment for your eyes so you will be able to see. I correct and discipline everyone I love. So be diligent and turn from your indifference. Look! I stand at the door and knock. If you hear my voice and open the door, I will come in, and we will share a meal together as friends."* – Revelation 3:15-20 NLT

The believers in the church of Laodicea had backslidden to the point that they didn't even see their own true condition. They may have had worldly success and prosperity, but Jesus called out their spiritual state. In terms of their spiritual condition, they were wretched, miserable, poor, blind, and naked before Him. He referred to them as being "lukewarm." The term or word lukewarm is a metaphor based on the quality of the water supply in Laodicea. Hierapolis was a nearby city famous for its hot, therapeutic mineral springs. Its water was delivered by aqueduct to Laodicea. However, the water would cool to a lukewarm temperature during its journey, losing much of its rich, useful, and even healing qualities. Colossae was another nearby city, and it was known for its mountain springs of cold, fresh, invigorating water. Jesus said that the believers in Laodicea were neither hot nor cold, and He wished they were one or the other. The Message Bible uses the words "stale" and "stagnant." The spiritual condition of these believers was sickening to God. They had become useless in the Kingdom of God. Jesus urged them to turn from their indifference and turn back to a place of being passionate and zealous for Him. Although the believers had erred in their ways, Jesus was willing to restore them. In fact, He said the rebuke and warning He was bringing to them was coming out of the place of His own yearning love for them. His words were spoken out of His passionate desire to be united with them.

> *The people I love, I call to account—prod and correct and guide so that they'll live at their best. Up on your feet, then! About face! Run after God! Look at me. I stand at the door. I knock. If you hear me call and open the door, I'll come right in and sit down to supper with you. – Revelation 3:19-20 MSG*

He was calling the believers in Laodicea to repentance. He was urging them to return to a close, love relationship with Him. This "knocking" represents the prodding of God speaking to the believer's heart through His Word and through the voice of His Spirit. This "door" represents the door of the believer's heart. He promises to fellowship with anyone who will heed His voice and welcome Him. This invitation reaches far beyond the limits of the body of believers at Laodicea. The language used here may be understood as applicable to all people. Jesus is inviting us to give Him entrance that we might enjoy the fullness of life and joy in His glorious presence. Joseph Benson describes this as an invitation to "loving fellowship, of quiet repose, of absolute satisfaction of all desires and needs, which will be ours if we open the door of our hearts by faith and let Jesus come in." The promise to come in and sup with us is an image denoting intimacy and friendship. Albert Barnes says that this language speaks of a "close, familiar, happy communication" between Christ and us.

> *I will come right in and sit down to supper with you. – Revelation 3:20b MSG*

"Supper" at this time and in this culture was considered the main social meal. In all countries and all cultures throughout time, sitting down to a meal together has always been a symbol of friendship and fellowship. The idea being communicated in Revelation 3:20 is that those who receive Christ can have this kind of intimacy that is shared between friends. The sentiment expressed within these words is one of sitting down to a friendly and cherished meal together. This is what Jesus is promising here. We have an opportunity to enjoy a personal, close-knit relationship with Jesus. Those who open their hearts and lives to him have the privilege of enjoying His presence. Open the door of your heart that He may come in and feast with you and you with Him! If you have never opened that door and asked Him to come in, do it today. If you have drifted away from this one central thing, return with a renewed passion and zeal. To the one who has been faithfully abiding with the Lord, lean in closer. Let nothing pull you away from spending time with Jesus. Do not allow anything that you may face on your life's journey to cause you to become lukewarm. Difficulties and troubles have the potential to either distract you or drive you right to the secret place with God. Choose the secret place! The sweet fellowship with Jesus, the most beautiful communion with the one we love—it really is the main ingredient in the right recipe. It is in the place of His glorious presence that we find all that fills our hearts. It's in the place of sitting at His feet, drinking from His cup, and feasting at His table.

I've found the recipe for being happy. – Philippians 4:12b MSG

 MY PRAYER FOR YOU

May He grant you, out of the riches of His glory, to be strengthened and spiritually energized with power through His Spirit in your inner self, [indwelling your innermost being and personality], so that Christ may dwell in your hearts through your faith. And may you, having been [deeply] rooted and [securely] grounded in love, be fully capable of comprehending with all the saints (God's people) the width and length and height and depth of His love [fully experiencing that amazing, endless love]; and [that you may come] to know [practically, through personal experience] that love of Christ which far surpasses [mere] knowledge (without experience), that you may be filled up [throughout your being] to all the fullness of God [so that you may have the richest experience of God's presence in your lives, completely filled and flooded with God Himself]. – Ephesians 3:16-19 AMP

NOTES

Day One: Guard Clear Thinking with Your Life

1. Definitions from Oxford Languages; smoke screen
2. A. Blomfield, *Sermons in Town and Country*, p. 193.
3. Brown-Driver-Briggs, Hebrew Definitions; Heart
4. Strong's Hebrew and Greek Dictionary, H320; Heart
5. Thayer's Greek Definitions, G5590; Soul
6. John Wesley's Explanatory Notes; Luke 21:1

Day Two: Pull Down Those Strongholds

1. Albert Barnes' Notes on the Bible; 2 Corinthians 10:4
2. Thayer's Greek Definitions, G2480; Do
3. Strong's Hebrew and Greek Definitions, G2407; Cast down
4. Alfred Blomfield, *Sermons in Town and Country*, J. and C. Mozley, 1871, p. 196.
5. Earl Nightingale; *It 's Do-able!: Power to Unleash Your Dream*, Author House, 1 April 2013, p. 128.

Day Three: Fresh Perspective

1. Brown-Driver-Briggs' Hebrew Definitions, Isaiah 26:3; Yetser (steadfast mind)
2. The Pulpit Commentary; Philippians 4:8
3. A. Blomfield, *Sermons in Town and Country*, p. 193.

Day Four: A Contented Mind is a Continual Feast

1. The Pulpit Commentary, Homilies by R. M. Edgar, *The art of Divine content*; Philippians 4:11
2. The Jamieson, Fausset, and Brown's Commentary on the Whole Bible, Philippians 4:11; I
3. Albert Barnes' Notes on the Bible, 1 Timothy 6:6; Contentment
4. Farlex Dictionary of Idioms; "A contented mind is a continual feast."
5. Ellicott's Commentary for the English Reader, Proverbs 15:15; Afflicted
6. The Pulpit Commentary, Proverbs 15:15; Afflicted
7. Strong's Hebrew and Greek Definitions, H3820; Labe (heart)
8. Thayer's Greek Definitions, H3820; Labe (heart)

Day 5: Count it all Joy

1. Strong's Hebrew and Greek Definitions, James: 1:25; Makarios (blessed)
2. H. Allon, *The Indwelling Christ*, p. 107.

Day 7: Receive Good Seed

1. Albert Barnes' Notes on the Bible; 1 Peter 1:23
2. Matthew Henry's Commentary on the Whole Bible; Matthew 13:3-9, 18-23

Day 8: Springing Up with New Life

1. Strong's Hebrew and Greek Definitions; Babes
2. Billy Graham, *Hope for Each Day*; https://billygrahamlibrary.org/read-the-bible-in-a-year-october-2016/
3. Commentary on Galatians, Luther Classic Commentaries, p. 19.

Day 9: Full of Sap

1. Strong's Hebrew and Greek Definitions, H835; 'esher (blessed)
2. Matthew Henry's Commentary on the Whole Bible; Psalm 1:1
3. Brown-Driver-Briggs' Definitions, Psalm 1:3, tsalach (prosper)
4. John Gill's Exposition of the Entire Bible, John 7:37-38; Living water

Day 10: Press On

1. Strong's Hebrew and Greek Definitions, H7488; Green
2. Thayer's Greek-English Lexicon of the New Testament, G4657; Dung

Day 11: Stronger with Every Step Forward

1. The Passion Translation 2020 edition, Broad Street Publishing, Hebrews 12:1, footnote f.
2. Strong's Hebrew and Greek Definitions, G591; Yields
3. Thayer's Greek Definitions, G591; Yields

Day 12: Courageous Self-Recovery in God's Strength

1. Strong's Hebrew and Greek Definitions, G3886; Feeble
2. The Pulpit Commentary, Hebrews 12:12; anorthoo (strengthen)
3. Thayer's Greek Definitions, Hebrews 12:13; ektrepo (put out of joint)
4. Albert Barnes' Notes on the Bible; Hebrews 12:12-14
5. Ray C. Stedman, IVP New Testament Commentary Series; Hebrews 12
6. Thayer's Greek Definitions, G2390; Healed

Day 13: Fresh and Flourishing

1. Strong's Hebrew and Greek Definitions, H6524; Flourish
2. Thayer's Greek Definitions, H6524; Flourish
3. Adam Clarke's Commentary on the Bible, Psalm 92:12; William Lithgow, Lithgow's 17 years' Travels, 4to., London, 1640
4. Matthew Henry's Commentary on the Whole Bible; Psalm 92:12-14
5. Albert Barnes' Notes on the Bible, Psalm 92:12; Dr. Thomson, *Land and the Book*, vol. i.

Day 14: Store Up the Word of God

1. Brown-Driver-Briggs' Hebrew Definitions, H6845; Hidden
2. John Gill's Exposition of the Entire Bible; Psalm 119:11
3. John Darby's Synopsis; Hebrews 4:12

4. Amplified Bible, 2015 edition, The Lockman Foundation, Hebrews 4:12, footnote a. (scalpel)
5. Matthew Henry's Commentary on the Whole Bible; Hebrews 4:12

Day 15: His Word Out of Your Mouth

1. Brown-Driver-Briggs' Hebrew Definitions, Psalm 1:3, H1897; Meditate
2. Strong's Hebrew and Greek Definitions, Psalm 1:3, H1897; Meditate
3. Strong's Hebrew and Greek Definitions, Matthew 12:36-37, G692; Idle Word
4. The Passion Translation 2020 edition, Broad Street Publishing, Matthew 12:36-37, footnote h.
5. Strong's Hebrew and Greek Definitions, Proverbs 18:21, H3027; Power
6. Thayer's Greek Definitions, Hebrews 4:12 and Revelations 1:16, G1366; Two-edged
7. The Passion Translation 2020 edition, Broad Street Publishing, Hebrews 4:12, footnote h. (two-mouthed)
8. https://biblehub.com/greek/1366.htm, Hebrews 4:12 and Revelations 1:16; G1366
9. The Pulpit Commentary, S.R. Aldridge; Romans 10

Day 16: An Energizing Force

1. New Spirit-Filled Life Bible, 2002, Thomas Nelson Inc, Kingdom Dynamics, p. 1322. (Seed Faith, Oral Roberts)
2. Matthew Henry's Commentary on the Whole Bible; Matthew 8

Day 17: Moving from Worry to Faith

1. Henry Allon, *The Indwelling Christ and Other Sermons,* Bible House 1892; p. 111.
2. Strong's Hebrew and Greek Definitions, James 1:8; Hodos (Ways)
3. Strong's Hebrew and Greek Definitions, Philippians 4:7; Peace

Day 18: Cling to the Lord and Hold Fast

1. https://www.webster-dictionary.org/definition/Trust
2. Brown-Driver-Briggs' Hebrew Definitions, H982; Batach (trust)
3. Brown-Driver-Briggs' Hebrew Definitions, H3045; Yada (acknowledge)
4. Alexander MacLaren, MacLaren's Commentary- Expositions of Holy Scripture; Trust

Day 19: Adapt

1. Oxford Languages; resilient
2. https://dictionary.cambridge.org/us/dictionary/english/resilient
3. https://www.dictionary.com/browse/resilient

Day 20: Walking in Wisdom

1. The Pulpit Commentary; Ecclesiastes 3
2. The Sermon Bible Commentary; Proverbs 3:5-6
3. Thayer's Greek-English Lexicon of the New Testament; Righteousness
4. J. Vaughan, Forty Sermons, 4th series, p. 286.

Day 21: Finding Purpose

    1. *The Complete Works of C. H. Spurgeon*, Volume 32: Sermons 1877-1937
    2. Brown-Driver-Briggs' Hebrew Definitions, H2165; Season
    3. Strong's Hebrew and Greek Definitions, H6256; Time
    4. Adam Clarkes' Commentary on the Bible; Ecclesiastes 3:11
    5. Strong's Hebrew and Greek Definitions, H7200; Perceive
    6. Adam Clarke's Commentary on the Bible; Ecclesiastes 3:22
    7. Spurgeon's Verse Expositions of the Bible, *The Sermon of Seasons*, March 14, 1886; Genesis 8:22

Day 22: Rejoice

    1. H. W. Beecher, *Christian World Pulpit*, vol. xiv., p. 313
    2. Strong's Hebrew and Greek Definitions, G2169; Eucharistia (Thanksgiving)
    3. Strong's Hebrew and Greek Definitions, G5463; Chairo (Rejoice)
    4. Thayer's Greek Definitions, G5463; Chairo (Rejoice)
    5. Albert Barnes' Notes on the Bible; Philippians 4:4
    6. Sermon Bible Commentary, John 15:11, H. Alford; *Quebec Chapel Sermons*, vol. ii., p. 280.

Day 23: A Strong Resolve

    1. John Gill's Exposition of the Entire Bible; Psalm 52:8

Day 24: Anointed in His Presence

    1. The Jamieson, Fausset, and Brown's Commentary on the Whole Bible; Psalm 52:8

Day 25: Arise

    1. *The Fruit of Christ's Presence*, Harry Lee Poe, pp 21-22.

Day 26: Vital Union with Christ

    1. *The True Vine*, Andrew Murray, 1898

Day 27: Eat and Drink

    1. Thayer's Greek Definitions, G2222; Life (Zoe)
    2. Thayer's Greek Definitions, G2198; Living (Zao)

Day 28: An Invited Guest

    1. The Passion Translation 2020 edition, Broad Street Publishing, John 15:16, footnote c.
    2. The Jamieson, Fausset, and Brown's Commentary on the Whole Bible; John 10:10
    3. Thayer's Greek Definitions, G4053; Abundantly
    4. J. Oswald Dykes, Christian World Pulpit, vol. xxiv., p. 177.
    5. Strong's Hebrew and Greek Definitions, G5479; Chara (Joy)
    6. Matthew Henry's Commentary on the Whole Bible; John 15:12-13
    7. Adam Clarke's Commentary on the Bible; Matthew 15:11

Day 29: Come Closer

1. John Gill's Exposition of the Entire Bible; Proverbs 17:22
2. Adam Clarke's Commentary on the Bible; Proverbs 17:22
3. Brown-Driver-Briggs' Hebrew Definitions, H5315; Soul
4. Brown-Driver-Briggs' Hebrew Definitions, H2421; Live
5. The Expositor's Bible Commentary; John 4:7
6. Strong's Hebrew and Greek Definitions, H1980; Come

Day 30: The Main Course

1. Albert Barnes' Notes on the Whole Bible; 1 Peter 1:6

Closing: From the Shadows to the Substance

1. Benson's Commentary on the Old and New Testaments; Revelations 3:19-20
2. Albert Barnes' Notes on the Bible; Revelations 3:19-20

ABOUT THE AUTHOR

Jennifer Rash resides in South Carolina and has served the Lord in many different capacities over the last 33 years. Jennifer is an ordained minister, coach, and mentor. She has a heart for women's ministry, leading women's conferences, Bible studies, women's groups, and mentoring young women. Jennifer has traveled across the country speaking to women's groups and pouring into women of all walks of life. There is a passion within her to see women reach their full potential. And her focus is on the health and vitality of the whole woman, spirit, soul, and body. Visit JenniferRash.com for more books, resources, and leader's guides for group study.

Made in the USA
Columbia, SC
17 May 2022

60560720R00111